SURVIVE, ADAPT, SUCCEED IN TODAY'S WORKPLACE

William Alexandre

SURVIVE, ADAPT, SUCCEED IN TODAY'S WORKPLACE

What if being an employee in a crisis was the chance of your lifetime?

Great Midlands
PUBLISHING

ISBN 978-1-916702-17-2

william-alexandre.com

Translation : Graham MacLachlan
www.mactrad.fr

Cover design: Patrick Grimaldi
www.patrickgrimaldi.net

Contents

To all those who have appreciated, helped and supported me

To all those who have loathed, demeaned, humiliated and betrayed me

Without you, I would never have made it

Thank you

Introduction

Do you look forward to going to work in the morning? You do? Well, if that really is the case, then you are part of a happy minority. Recently I read an eye-opening article on a study which concluded that for more than nine out of ten employees, the answer was a resounding "No". But do we really need studies and statistics to tell us what most of us already know through personal experience or from what those close to us actually say?

So who looks forward to going to work in the morning? Who can possibly look forward to the daily slog for a salary which, once taxes, monthly repayments, bills, school fees and all the other expenses have been paid, leaves very little for anything else? Who can possibly look forward to spending every day with people who aren't particularly likeable, and with bosses who can be ungrateful and maybe even create a stressful and toxic atmosphere to further their personal ambitions? Who can possibly look forward to keeping a low profile and dissimulating their personality – even abandoning their dignity on occasion – for fear of missing out on a bonus or losing their job?

Unemployment. That sword of Damocles which at any time can strike any employee, whether excellent or mediocre, the most hard-working or the laziest, the most trustworthy or the most disloyal. That sword of Damocles which leaves you submerged by your financial obligations, excluded from established circles, estranged from your friends and sometimes even your own family, and which can pull the rug from under your feet and leave you broken inside.

I know plenty of people who have been unemployed. Employees, skilled technicians, engineers, even directors of big businesses listed on the stock market. School dunces and kids that came top of the class. Drop-outs and graduates from some of the most prestigious schools on the planet. Employees of modest companies as well as those of supposedly too-big-to-fail corporations. Newcomers and old hands. No salaried employee is ever entirely safe from being laid off. Not a single one.

The risk is even greater the older you get and the more intense the global competition becomes. Few westerners realize, for example, just how many civil engineering projects (roads, railways, etc.) are now designed and coordinated from countries such as India, Tunisia and Eastern Europe... Artificial intelligence is progressing in leaps and bounds and poses a threat to those of us whose tasks, whether skilled or otherwise, tend to be repetitive. Cash-strapped states and under-funded retirement schemes are forcing us to work longer. That's true. But what can you do when companies try to rid themselves of the over 50s so they can hire younger workers? And of course one day the young will reach 50 too...

How can you enjoy your career to the full as a salaried employee? How can you increase your peace of mind, comfort and independence?

Obviously the ideal solution is to be financially independent. Some books on this subject are excellent and help change the lives of their readers in a positive way. Including this one, I might add (with a smile).

But here's the thing. The ideal solution isn't so easy to put into practice. Firstly, starting a business just isn't for everyone. You need to have an idea that is economically viable, and that is not as easy as it sounds.

Next, you need capital. But what do you do when your savings amount at best to a few years' salary which your family will have to live off if you lose your job or have to deal with an unexpected event? Are you really prepared to put your children's education at risk? How do you accumulate a significant amount of savings with all the taxes, financial expenses and household costs you have to pay?

You also need time. But where do you find it when every day you are working seven or eight hours, spending a couple of hours on public transport or in the car, and contributing to family activities too? Free time at the weekend is often in short supply for the family and in even shorter supply for yourself.

You also need inspiration and luck. Some find that inspiration when they are 20, others at 50, and yet more never find it all. As for luck, unfortunately it does not always turn up at the right moment...

And of course you need courage. Courage to overcome your fears, some of which are deeply ingrained, such as the fear of failure or criticism. Courage to tackle the inner demons or mistaken beliefs that are holding you back. Courage (or foolhardiness) to accept losing the little you have already acquired in the hope of achieving some elusive profit.

Gaining independence is easier said than done and, for many, a salaried position is (unfortunately) the only realistic option available.

So what's special about this one employee in ten who looks forward to going to work in the morning?

Allow me to tell you – briefly – the story of a regular guy I know very well.

He was born into a middle-class family. His parents worked in a bank. He had a relatively happy childhood without being too spoilt. He was rather shy, self-conscious and somewhat withdrawn. He felt more comfortable in the company of a computer than girls, who both attracted and intimidated him. He didn't have the confidence of other boys, those bad boys who fascinate teenage girls and whose success arouses envy in the less fortunate.

At school he was an average student, even rather a poor one in certain subjects such as chemistry and physics. As for sport, he was a hopeless case. On the bright side, he developed an interest in economics, history and mathematics, and the prospect of studying economics at university appealed to him. And yet his teachers and careers advisers poured cold water on the idea, telling him repeatedly that he wasn't cut out for studying and should think about taking a short vocational course and entering the workplace rapidly.

Stubborn by nature, he ignored their advice and signed up for an economics course, working nights to catch up. Two years later he got into the most prestigious university for economics and management in the country. A few more years, and he left with a master's in finance and another in economics.

His career got off to a reasonable start, but he soon found himself out of work. He realized that his qualifications were not going to protect him from the unemployment aisles, and that the competition was fierce. He went to London to work for a prestigious British financial group and five years later found himself once again out of work. Working menial jobs to make ends meet, he tried to set up his own business using the skills he had already acquired but success was not forthcoming. He felt like a loser more than ever, and was ready to call it a day.

He resigned himself to looking for a new job and was hired as a senior manager in one of the largest engineering companies in the world. A year later, a major oil company offered him a position in Switzerland, tripling his salary in the process.

Another four years went by and the same company promoted him to its international headquarters, once again tripling his salary.

In just six years this regular guy managed to multiply a senior manager's salary by nine, despite having once been on the minimum wage and unemployment benefits. In the interlude, he helped this major oil company generate more than 300 million dollars...

This regular guy wasn't a loser. He was no longer an expense, a burden for his employers. He had set about generating more, much more, than he cost. He was no longer an expense or a burden, but a very profitable investment. He was no longer a loser, but an authority recognized in his field for his expertise and leadership, no longer saving just forty dollars on his heating bill, but charging over two thousand dollars a day.

That regular guy was, of course, me.

In this book, I won't be trying to sell you pipe dreams. For the simple reason that I don't have any to sell. I won't try to sell you a miracle solution either. For the same reason. No. In this book I just want to share with you the fundamental lessons that my career has taught me, the lessons that have borne fruit, because I would not wish on anyone the experience of unemployment and its attendant fear and suffering.

Today, I no longer live in fear of losing my job and I am a happy employee who lives comfortably and every day a little better. Not only have I learnt to protect myself from getting laid off, I also feel useful and happy as an employee.

These fundamental lessons that my personal experience has taught me, I want to share with you. I see far too many people, regardless of their rank, qualifications, salary or experience, who aren't happy at work and it is a sight I find hard to bear. Even more so because I have experienced it myself, because the general trend in our economies and societies is for ever greater job insecurity.

How many have, despite their good intentions and inner zeal, seen their enthusiasm in the workplace wane as the years go by? How many have been demotivated by a lack of recognition and respect from their hierarchy? How many have been demotivated by the negligence of certain colleagues who have twigged that they can do less and still earn the same, if not more? How many would like to see if the grass is greener elsewhere? But greener grass is in short supply and often you just have to make the most of the situation, even if that means abandoning some of your values.

I have read books, watched videos and spoken to "coaches" and "experts", self-help professionals and career advisers who, for the most part, have never been anything but a cost burden for their previous employers. Some even offer tips on surviving in a company when they have never worked or generated a cent for a company, and might even be unemployed... When you are efficient, when you generate money, especially lots of money, your employer will as a general rule keep you on and try by every means to extend your employment. Anyone with an ounce of nous would never cook the goose who lays the golden eggs...

It was these fake experts who provided me with another reason for writing this book. The words in this book are born from real success. Not the success of another. My success, and only my success.

A desire to do something useful drove me to write these lines. It feels good to being doing something useful, to be able to tell one's story in the hope that it might benefit those who happen to read it. Who doesn't enjoy telling, for example, their children stories drawn from personal experience in the hope that they might learn a useful life lesson?

I hope you will find my experience useful, that this book will help improve your well-being as you go about your professional activities.

To make this book as easy to read as possible I have divided it into several parts, each being a prerequisite for understanding the next. First of all we need to clarify what exactly a company is and discard once and for all the myths and legends which cause so much disappointment to so many. You need to be able to see and accept the reality of your professional situation if you are to avoid severe disillusionment in the workplace.

Next, it is very important that you have a strong profile. A strong profile involves a combination of expertise, technique and experience, as well as all the strong human values, soft skills and a special frame of mind.

Once you have developed a strong profile, or start to develop one, you need to take action. And I mean taking action, not just wishing, dreaming, imagining or fantasizing. But taking action is not enough, because the actions you take need to be done properly. Which is why we will spend time looking at what you can actually undertake and how you can go about undertaking it. Actions that have been properly studied, properly targeted and properly performed are nearly always successful. By following these self-same principles I have managed to bring to fruition almost all of my actions. I put a limit on how many I undertake, generally just a few, and then focus all my energy on the ones I am prioritizing.

Nevertheless any success is always fragile and you need to know how to exploit it otherwise someone else will exploit it in your stead, and you will usually realize this too late to do anything about it. So I will share with you my principles and techniques for not only exploiting your successes but also capitalizing on them.

Lastly, I will tackle the subject of financial independence. For some, this is a goal they have already achieved. For others, it is an unattainable dream or an ideal they have channelled into other activities. Everyone dreams of financial independence because it is the only way to entirely avoid that grim sword of Damocles we call unemployment. It is the only way of being able to choose whether you work or not, for what, for whom and how.

My experience has taught me how to survive in the workplace and enjoy my job. And by helping my employer generate millions of extra dollars a year, my experience has also enabled me, albeit indirectly, to multiply my previous salary by a factor of no less than nine. This additional income not only pays for a better lifestyle, it has also allowed me to set aside a considerable amount in savings and has set me on the road to achieving financial independence. By learning to survive and progress in the workplace, I have allowed a bridge to develop between my own situation in life and the holy grail of a comfortable retirement. Every year I take a few more steps across this bridge. What seemed unattainable ten years ago has rather easily and naturally come to pass.

My experience has made me appreciate being an employee again. I have taken back control of my life and today, without any particular effort, I am heading towards that affluent destination which everyone dreams of. It feels like I am being carried along by a current that is both energizing and soothing. In sharing with you the fundamental lessons that I have been able to draw from my years of experience, I hope that you too will flourish professionally and enjoy swimming in the pleasant stream which flows towards financial independence.

1
The Workplace
or
One for All, and Every Man for Himself

Many people develop a very subjective view of the workplace, either idealizing or demonizing it. For your personal strategy to be successful, you really need to understand the environment you are working in. This means considering the facts impartially and analysing them rationally. If you rely on assumptions, dreams and emotions to get you through the working day, you will be seriously disappointed.

Avoiding disappointment is essential. If you idealize an environment that is, in reality, much harsher than you imagine, you will suffer. On the other hand, you might end up feeling frustrated if you demonize, abandon or underestimate the potential of an environment that is teeming with opportunities.

Also you need to develop and maintain your values – those principles and standards that make you who you are – in an environment which sometimes forces people to renounce all or part of what it is that makes them human. By bearing in mind the harsh reality of the environment you work in, you will not only preserve your values but also develop the traits which will make you a fully paid-up member of the human race.

So in this opening chapter we shall set the scene as it really is, and remind ourselves of the basics.

1.1
Companies focus on making money, not on social issues

A company is by definition a legal entity whose purpose is to make profits or savings. Nothing else.

This means you need to keep your feet squarely on the ground. It isn't a friendship club, it isn't a large family, it isn't a social organization which owes you something without you giving it anything in exchange.

Your relationship with your company is defined very simply. It is your contract of employment. You work a certain number of hours for a given task or according to a job description. In return you get paid. And that's it. No more, no less.

Always keep this in mind, whatever your position, whatever your rank and whatever the size of your salary. You owe nothing more to your company than what you agreed to in your contract. Your company owes you nothing more than what it agreed to in your contract.

Your contract of employment is a deal. And a professional sticks to the deal they sign.

That's the number one rule.

1.2
You are not indispensable

Apart from a few exceptional cases, your company existed before you joined it. It can continue to exist and operate without you. In fact it most certainly will continue to exist and operate without you. From the lowliest worker to the chief executive officer, including engineers and accountants, everyone can be replaced. Every single one.

Do you think you can do special things? Do you think that the organization you put together makes you indispensable and without you, everything will grind to a halt? Don't worry. Your colleagues will adapt and even if the tasks won't be done so well, they will get them done. Your absence will be a little headache for a few weeks, perhaps for a few months at most.

Look around you. Does your company stop when someone retires, resigns, has a baby or takes sick leave? Of course not. When somebody leaves a company, it isn't unusual to see a flock of office vultures strip the last remnants from their work station. Stapler, computer screen or whatever else can be reused is taken. And who remembers the employee who worked at that desk three months ago? What was he called? Few of his old colleagues even remember his name.

On the contrary, as an employee, your company is truly indispensable to you. Without it, you don't have a salary.

1.3
Me first, then everybody else

Whether we like it or not, human nature is selfish. Being selfish isn't necessarily negative. Before thinking of your colleagues' well-being, you obviously think about your own and your survival.

I have experienced crises that involved mass redundancies. Overnight, yesterday's friendly colleagues turned into formidable and merciless rivals, even to the point of facilitating their neighbour's mistakes so the latter got the push first, instead of them. The nice, fatherly manager turned into a pitiless warrior hunting for scalps, eliminating one by one the members of his team. Team spirit, much extolled and immortalized in numerous team-building photos, was elbowed aside by a law of the jungle of the most ferocious type imaginable. Anyone who has experienced a redundancy scheme will know what I am talking about.

So you should put yourself first. And that is nothing to be ashamed of. You might well have scruples, but do you think your colleagues will put your well-being before their own?

We will see later in this book that, even though you should put yourself first every time, your success in the workplace will depend largely on your ability to make your interests align not only with those of your company, but also with those of your colleagues.

1.4
You serve your bosses first

A company is an artificial person. It doesn't think, it doesn't make decisions, it doesn't hire, promote or fire. It is a legal entity which only exists on the company register.

However your boss can influence decisions, and perhaps he or she can even make the decision to hire, promote or fire you. And their boss can do the same to them. The executive committee is also appointed, or dismissed, by the shareholders and its bonuses are decided by the remuneration committee.

In short, everyone has a boss. You are responsible to yours, who is responsible to his or hers, and so on.

Achieving success in your career depends greatly on your ability to provide your bosses with the means to impress theirs. You have to make sure that every rank above you benefits, right up to the directors and the shareholders. Without you getting swindled, obviously.

Gratitude isn't a natural quality in the workplace, like it isn't in the political arena. On the contrary, it is a rare thing. So if you don't want to see your boss take the credit for all your hard work, beware of underhand tricks and false promises. And that's not all.

A large part of this book is devoted to helping you provide added value to your company's hierarchy, while making sure you also benefit and keep the risks under control. Successfully implementing this step is fundamental to your progress. Without it, not only do you considerably increase the risks that threaten your survival, but you also eliminate almost every chance of enjoying an efficient career development.

Lastly, don't forget the old saying: "Never bite the hand that feeds you."

1.5
You'll have more enemies than friends around you

The workplace is the modern equivalent of the jungle. Danger is everywhere. And yet everything appears to be the epitome of peace and harmony. This cosy environment full of friendly, smiling people, governed by a code of ethics, regulated by procedures and managed by a considerate boss who regularly asks after the latest addition to the family, does indeed feel safe and comforting. But that's just your perception, an illusion that should never be allowed to divert your attention from the dangers prowling around the workplace. These dangers are, for you, a constant threat.

Human nature is what it is, and you will never change it. Everyone has sweetness in them, and also a darker side. You just have to find common ground and, above all, have no illusions.

This implies that the people in the office around you are normal, despite their diverse range of profiles. Most of them will not judge you in a rational way but on the emotions you arouse within them.

Jealousy is a powerful creator of enemies within company walls. Did you get the job that someone else was coveting? Is your car or your spouse better looking than your colleague's? Do you have a bigger house? Are your children doing well at school? Do you seem happy? Well, it is very likely that your success and happiness is irritating the mean-minded and envious in your surroundings. Your team, your colleagues, your managers and even your big boss can potentially be envious of your situation, and what's more, people can be very good at hiding it. So you are going to have to manage the envious, understand how to put them to good use, manage the associated risks (rumours, mistakes in a report, etc.) and turn them into followers. We'll come back to this aspect later in the book.

Desire is another powerful creator of enemies, and closely linked to jealousy. The difference is that desire isn't a simple feeling like jealousy. Desire creates a goal that the desirer will endeavour to attain through actions which can sometimes be of an unexpected nature. Someone who desires your job will do everything in their power to make you fail. A superior in search of success could desire yours, if you have achieved some.

Just like the jealous, desirers can be absolutely anyone and hide behind the mask of someone who is nice and trustworthy. Similarly, you can turn desirers into followers by transforming their toxicity into a positive power. And once again, I'll do my best to explain how you can do that.

Gossipers and other bearers of malicious news can also be a hindrance and even dangerous. Turn them into followers, too – but also keep them handy to be used for your own communication needs. We'll come back to this point.

Rotten apples, smooth talkers, skivers, liars and their ilk are all dangerous but only if you haven't identified their true traits and are counting on them. Their inaction, often exacerbated by a lack of real competencies, means you can never rely on them. Just try to spot them to improve your chances of not falling into their trap in the future.

In some companies you'll find warring clans. Don't join a clan. They can cost you dearly. Even if one clan appears to be losing ground to another, a last-minute reversal of fortunes is always possible. Stay neutral. Serve all members of both clans without discrimination and with the same professionalism. You are a professional who doesn't take sides, and this attitude will gain you the confidence and trust of each clan. Regardless of which clan wins in the end.

Don't forget your goals: survive and progress.

Your enemies will do their best to trip you up. Your time and energy are precious commodities, so don't waste them on pointless battles which will wear you down and perhaps one day prove to be your undoing. Instead, reserve your energy for the next steps and convert your enemies into either supporters or followers.

1.6
What seems to be illogical or stupid rarely is

Who hasn't had to deal with some absurd situation in the workplace? Whether you are an employee, business partner or customer, at some time or another you must have experienced unbelievable, even preposterous situations which have given rise to some memorable belly laughs.

However certain unbelievable situations end up as tragedies. How many high-level managers have taken what seem to be illogical and stupid decisions that result in huge losses or even bankruptcy for their company? When this occurs in a large group, the opinions begin to fly. How did someone in such a high-ranking position make such an ill-considered choice? This is tantamount to armchair analysis and is as easy to do as identifying the mistakes of generals which led to a military defeat some 100 years ago...

Commenting or voicing an opinion is easy. No experience or particular ability is required. Consequently everybody and anybody is capable of having a view on events. But understanding precisely what caused a situation or an action requires much more effort.

All "stupid" situations and actions are the result of a logical progression. They are often the consequence of an incomplete or inexact piece of information. For any number of reasons (no time, lack of resources, inexperience, etc.), the person who caused a given situation probably did not have all the necessary information they needed to make the right decision. A report or a percentage might also have turned out to be wrong. Sometimes events only offer a choice between bad options, and in such cases you have to choose the least damaging.

Unfortunately such errors often have serious consequences for a company. They can waste the time of its employees, they can transform its investments into losses, they can scare away its customers and prospects... In short, they will almost certainly cost the company money. And making money is the whole point of a company.

Such errors are, therefore, excellent opportunities that need to be taken advantage of. Understanding the mechanism which caused them, putting a figure on the cost or loss of potential earnings, and bringing to the table a concrete solution are all sure-fire ways for you to score a few points with your colleagues. You will gain the respect of all those who suffered in the event.

The bottom line is that nothing is stupid or illogical. If something does indeed appear to be stupid or illogical, take a closer look. It might just be an opportunity for you.

1.7
Squeezing the lemon

What do you do when you squeeze a lemon? You keep the juice and throw the expended peel away.

When an acquaintance who brings you nothing but problems becomes an obstacle to your personal happiness, what do you do? In general, you keep your distance.

It is the same thing with an employee. As long as you've got tasks to do, as long as you can contribute to the wealth of the company, as long as your bosses benefit from your work, and as long as the company is in good health then you'll be a fertile lemon tree producing nice juicy lemons. Lemon-producing is good for your survival in the short and medium terms.

On the other hand, the situation gets risky if you were hired to do a specific task which is coming to an end. Is your company's overall performance deteriorating? Are you working in a unit or a sector which is steadily running out of steam? If that's the case, then you risk ending up being the lemon or part of a group of lemons which has been squeezed of all its juice.

A lemon that has been squeezed dry has a limited future in the workplace. And the workplace can sometimes blind its occupants to the reality of their situation. Some workplace lemons get squeezed by colleagues who don't quite realize that they too are of the citrus persuasion...

Survival in the workplace requires that you avoid being a lemon and especially one that has almost been squeezed dry.

While some enjoy being lemon squeezers, and feel safe in such a role, I personally dislike it for two very simple reasons. The first is a question of ethics, as I feel uncomfortable in a role that is at odds with my principles. The other reason is that once there are no lemons left to squeeze, the squeezer risks becoming the next lemon to get squeezed.

I prefer growing a lemon tree or, even better, developing a lemon-tree plantation where people are no longer squeezed to a pulp but where they too become lemon-tree growers. That way you bring more value to the company, in-house rivalries give way to cooperation and your opponents, benefiting from the results and job security you provide, become your followers.

In recent years I have spent a lot of my time planting lemon trees. I've never regretted it. My plantation contributes to generating millions of dollars every year and keeps my bosses satisfied. Years ago, I was a competitor. I got squeezed like a lemon. I wasn't living very well and the energy I had to expend just to survive was exhausting me and, over time, it put me in hospital. Today, I am no longer a competitor, I no longer get squeezed and I feel at peace. I don't worry and I sleep better. I have more free time for me and for those I love.

1.8
A machine for grinding people down

Repetitiveness, a lack of meaning, no prospects of advancement, and the application of business processes by newly graduated consultants are just some of the many factors that can make work boring, unappealing and tiring.

If on top of that you've got a petty-minded and ungrateful management which practises the art of divisiveness to maintain its authority, or requires staff to undertake meaningless tasks or "bullshit jobs", then your job can soon become a demotivating chore.

In some extreme cases moral or sexual harassment, favouritism, pitching employees against each other to fight for their positions, and the permanent threat of unemployment can make a job a living hell.

Certain companies will even go as far as infantilizing their employees, many of whom are experienced professionals. They install pinball machines and organize conferences which feature colouring sessions, brick-building games, balloon twisting... In recent years we have seen the rise of the "Chief Happiness Officer", a sort of occupational psychologist. It is the ultimate humiliation for a professional, regardless of their business or rank, to be treated like a child or as if there is something wrong with them.

Boredom, fatigue, pressure, fear and treating adults like children are the perfect ingredients for a personality-destroying cocktail. A glass a day of this beverage and you'll surely end up a zombie, as many employees do. Zombie employees have a special power which makes them act like chameleons. They mimic their boss and spend their time blending in with the decor so they won't draw attention to themselves. They also carry out stupid orders without the slightest discussion. Adopting the zombie technique will wear you out psychologically, morally and perhaps even physically. It will also bounce back to destroy your private life, your family. And when that happens, get ready for a stay in hospital or a descent into purgatory.

If you are reading this book, it is probably because the life of a sheep in the herd, the loss of dignity, the living in fear and humiliation weren't your choice. They were never mine either. The only solution is to take action so you no longer have to endure such treatment, or at least reduce it as much as possible.

I once tasted that destructive cocktail and immediately spat it out, its bitterness being too much for me to take. In some darker periods of my life I even tried to develop a taste for it, but without success. With hindsight, I don't regret a thing and my choice seems to have borne fruit over time. Those who operate on this destructive cocktail rarely achieve the level of results that I do. As for happiness – which is my primary goal – such adepts of bitterness seem to have given up on that virtue a long time ago.

A good professional who is also a good leader doesn't have to serve this cocktail to those around them, not even a single one of its ingredients. On the contrary, they prefer to celebrate the successes of their team over delicious food and a bottle of fine wine.

1.9
Opportunities are everywhere

"We've always done it this way and it works very well!" "We've been telling the management about the problem for years, but nobody has ever done anything about it." "It's because of the slump." "Customers can be picky and often send back the products." "We're short-handed." "We don't have the right people for the job." "We need to cut costs." "Our competitors are better than us..."

We've all heard phrases like these, and many others, at least once in our career. For the most part they are the expression of a fatalistic attitude: "That's the way it goes. We just have to put up with it. After all, it isn't my fault, and it isn't my job to solve these problems, I'm not paid for that."

For those of you who want to survive and progress, such fatalistic attitudes are in fact a goldmine. All these problems are each an opportunity to shine, to secure promotion and justify a rise.

First of all you need to identify the problems and make a list. Keep your ears open in the relaxation areas, chat with colleagues, have lunch with people from other departments, and talk to managers about the problems they might experience with your own department.

Once your inventory has been completed, keep it to yourself. Don't share it.

Look at each point in your list, one by one. Try to estimate the financial impact of each problem. It isn't difficult because everything in a company can be costed.

For example, an accountant wastes a lot of time checking transactions. You can easily find out the hourly rate for an accountant on the internet. If you manage to set up a system in a spreadsheet program such as Microsoft Excel to partially automate the checking of transactions so the accountant spends about 20% less time on the task, then you will have reduced wasted time by 20% and created a productivity gain of 20% on their salary. That 20% of time could be used for doing something else, and perhaps the accountant will stop complaining about being understaffed too.

Several years ago falling oil prices forced companies to increase production in order to maintain their level of turnover. Unfortunately production could not be increased without injecting cash, and the company I worked for didn't have the resources to invest. I remembered an old conversation I had had with one of the technical managers who complained about the recurrent stoppages in the production chain. Suddenly the thought popped into my head that, while we couldn't produce more, we could produce better.

So I looked at the daily production statistics for each site and each country. With the help of engineers and technicians in the field (note "in the field" and not "at head office") we linked the number of days when production stopped to the various problems encountered. The associated loss was easy to cost by multiplying the volume produced per hour by the number of hours stopped and then by the retail price. Next we looked at all the solutions that could be implemented simply and for a modest outlay. For each solution implemented, which stoppages could be avoided? It turned out that the resulting production gains amounted to millions of dollars a year. When compared to the cost of the actions, the return on investment varied between 300% and 500%. The members of our little workgroup had more than merited their salaries, and our results attracted the gratitude of the chief executive officer and several members of the executive committee.

Some of the actions were incredibly simple. For example, certain emergency-stop buttons got accidentally pressed several times a year. The complex nature of the production chain meant that every time this happened, it blocked the system for three or four hours, amounting to a loss of earnings in the region of $15,000. Four stoppages a year amounted to $60,000. By fitting covers to these buttons, which cost just a few dollars, the problem disappeared. Spending a few dollars to save $60,000 annually, or $300,000 over five years, or $600,000 over ten years... Simple, inexpensive solutions can turn out to be excellent investments. Once again thanks to some shrewd communication, the directors heard about this little feat and were delighted.

Let's take another look at our inventory of problems. Think carefully about the problems and order them according to the following factors:

– amount at stake (estimate),
– number of people impacted,
– importance for the hierarchy (if nobody is aware of the problem, you need to organize a good communication plan to make sure that changes), and
– difficulty/ease of implementing solutions (number of people involved, technical complexity, inhouse obstacles...).

You will start to have a clearer view of the situation and certain points will capture your attention. Give it time and thought, and gradually your will be able to outline a few action plans.

The harsher the work environment becomes, the more the people around you become fatalistic or lazy (perhaps both) and the less the organization functions properly. These are the perfect conditions for producing opportunities. Just like low-hanging fruit, all you have to do is take them.

You need to be opportunistic. This is imperative. I love this word "opportunistic" and yet many folks give it a negative connotation which it doesn't deserve at all. For me, it is your frame of mind that gives opportunity its noble quality.

Opportunism in the negative sense is to benefit to the detriment of someone else. I call it "predatory opportunism" and it is malignant and pathetic.

Opportunism in the positive sense, in the way I think of it in my daily life, is to exploit the faults and problems to the benefit of the greatest number of people without harming anyone. In my two previous examples the team involved in the project benefited from the situation (including some people who had a very low profile in the organization), the production teams increased their results beyond the projections, and along the way we resolved a certain number of issues. The directors were proud to be able to announce an increase in turnover and profitable investments. As for me, the person who launched the initiative, I enjoyed the recognition of not only the company directors but also of those people who, at the time of joining the company, considered me to be yet another pen-pusher.

Opportunism like that doesn't harm anyone, quite the reverse. It is good for a large number of people and the general interest. It encourages people to take the initiative, produces tangible results for the company, and bestows recognition on some employees who might have otherwise been ignored for too long. Your sceptics and critics suddenly become allies, even followers. From now on your enemies will hesitate before attacking you and will probably look for easier targets instead.

Positive opportunism such as this also gives meaning to your work. It reawakens your appreciation for your professional life.

Be systematic in your opportunism, always in the best sense of the word. Always be on the lookout for opportunities to bring to fruition. Two or three worthwhile opportunities every year, carefully executed, will lead you to success and establish your reputation.

1.10
No pain, no gain

Nobody really likes this expression. Something more inspiring might be: "Get rich, do what you want, when you want, how you want, and without lifting a finger!" I am one of those happy optimists who buys copious lottery tickets in the hope of winning the big prize, much to the delight of the lottery shareholders and the government.

Life isn't easy, we all agree. Ordeals are more common than moments of pure happiness. Wishing, hoping and dreaming are all normal thought processes and everyone has them. We need hopes and dreams.

However waiting for dreams to materialize without doing anything to make them happen is the same as waiting to win fifty million dollars in the lottery from the comfort of your sofa. It might work, of course, but I'm sure you will readily agree that the likelihood of it happening is pretty low.

Surviving in the workplace requires effort. Progressing, even more so. You should be ready to learn, unlearn, challenge certain beliefs, face up to your doubts and fears, and overcome the discouraging words of those around you. You will experience periods of euphoria, moments of doubt, and times of despondency. This is normal. It is the lot of all those who want to succeed and all those who do succeed.

You will make mistakes. Once again, this is normal. Making a mistake is not the same thing as failure. You get better and learn from your mistakes and those of others. Your mistakes are opportunities for improving yourself. You are no longer at school where mistakes are systematically penalized. As the saying goes, only those who never do anything never make a mistake. Inactive and failure-free people are a twofold mistake for a company: the mistake of hiring them and the mistake of keeping them.

Personally, I make mistakes all the time, most of which are of no consequence. Thanks to my mistakes and my desire not to repeat them, I get better at my job every day. When I put them into perspective by comparing them to my successes, the results are there to reassure me. They are indisputable. And if I had to start over, I wouldn't change a thing.

Those results will dissipate the pain. I have never forgotten my difficult years, those years of struggling, nor where I come from. But today that all seems to me a bad and very distant memory. My life feels much more peaceful. That pain was a good pain, because it brought me happiness.

2
Having

In the previous chapter we reminded ourselves of certain realities in the workplace. Even if it is a difficult environment where egos reign supreme, it is also an environment which offers numerous opportunities for you to stand out, secure an income, foster your rise through the ranks, and make yourself useful to the community.

Now that the reminders have been made and the scene set, let's move on to what your prime consideration should be: preparing yourself mentally. The few principles that follow have always been a help to me. They have never let me down and, without them, I would never have made it.

2.1
Having dreams, a goal

Having a job is good. Earning a salary is good. Understanding why you work is even better.

Do you work so you can purchase a car or a house? Do you work in order to pay off a loan? Do you work so you can give your children a better start in life, hoping theirs will be better than yours? Do you work so you can provide for those you love and make them happy? Do you work in order to fund your retirement?

If that's the case, why do you continue to work once you've bought the car, paid for the house and nurtured your children to adulthood and independence? In other words, what will you do once you have retired?

You need to clarify your position on these questions if you haven't already done so.

In fact it can be dangerous to have as your main goal an intermediate goal, such as buying a house, because your life will continue after you've bought your house. Instead think about the reason behind your purchasing a house. Was it to provide an inheritance for your children? Put a roof over your head? Make your family happy? Impress your friends and family? All of the above?

Like any heritage item, for multiple reasons the price of your house can fluctuate upwards as well as downwards. If you lose your job, would you be able to cope with all your household expenses (mortgage, charges, maintenance, taxes, etc.) and thus remain safe under that roof of yours? Have you thought about the inheritance tax which your children will have to pay and which can, in some cases, easily eat up half the value of their inheritance? If this isn't the case, then perhaps you haven't entirely achieved your goal and still have some way to go. After all, I'm sure your aim wasn't to leave just 50% of your estate to your children and pay the other 50% in government taxes and solicitor's fees.

Intermediate goals are important, but they can often be confused with a life purpose. Whereas in fact they are just stages in life. And such stages need to be carefully studied. Working thirty years to pay off the mortgage on your house and then bequeathing it to your children in the hope that it puts them on a solid financial footing, is that such a shrewd plan? Once the interest has been paid to the bank, the inheritance taxes have been settled and the material depreciation has been taken into account, will the total price of the house provide your children with the financial security you hoped for? Perhaps by investing the total price of the house in another way you might be able to bequeath more, and more securely.

Bequeathing the family home to the children is just one example among many others. Everyone has their own reasons, motivations and beliefs.

More often than not we put our family first – our spouse, children, parents and friends. That's laudable. But what about you? Do you think about yourself? In all honesty, what kind of life would make you really happy? And what don't you like in your life? I don't think it would be a waste of time to sit down, alone, in a calm place, perhaps with a good bottle of wine or a hot cup of tea, and think carefully about these topics. We only live once and, instead of going to a happy grave, you risk taking with you a surfeit of regrets and sadness.

If you always put others first and yourself afterwards, there won't be any room for you. Put yourself first and then everybody else, ordering them according to their importance in your heart. Tough luck for the last ones if there isn't any room left.

Work should not be an inevitable obligation, but a means for achieving your goal. If you are lucky enough to have a clear objective in mind and you don't particularly enjoy your work, you are endowed with the most powerful motivation of all. Nothing will stop you.

By thinking about yourself, while taking care of all those you love and behaving with integrity, you will be a model for many of the people around you. First of all for your children, because they will see that their parent is happy, good at their work, principled, and takes care of them and those they love. You will leave behind a better memory than, "My parent slogged away throughout life for nothing." On the contrary, their memory will be, "My parent was principled, knew what they wanted, never gave up and always got there in the end. They were cheerful and devoted their time to achieving their passions. They loved us, we loved them, we admired them and if we are happy today, it's thanks to them." Personally I prefer the second option, don't you?

Many people around me have given up, live in their daydreams, live their lives vicariously through the lives of others because their own is completely empty. Others claim to be sacrificing themselves so that their children can have a better life.

Others take the opposite view. They have rolled up their sleeves and are getting on with finding the means and resources with which to realize their dreams. Their lives are exciting and full of projects. They try to understand, to learn and haven't got the time to concern themselves with other people's lives – unless they are genuinely interested and can learn something. They don't sacrifice themselves for anybody, not even their children. They don't soften. They don't attract pity. They succeed. Those that follow them succeed. Their children succeed and admire them.

As far as I'm concerned, my goal is to acquire both my intellectual and financial freedom. Intellectual, because I want to understand the subjects which are important to me and be able to reach an opinion by myself without stupidly repeating a marketing slogan, a politician's sound bite or a rumour. Financially, because I want to choose when I work and for whom I work, and do not experience the destructive stress that I suffered in the past.

Financially, because I also want my wife and children to enjoy the same freedom. Financial freedom enables you to buy time. The time I used to spend doing the household chores, cleaning and ironing, are now devoted to my real interests, such as history, cinema, philosophy, company projects, and writing books. I wouldn't have been able to support the causes I hold dear, either. Today I can and do support several charities devoted to the protection of animals. And when my family needs help, I no longer have to reply, "I'm sorry I can't".

We are all different and we all aspire to different things. Spending a bit of time identifying your ultimate goals is certainly one of the most fruitful investments you can ever make. Surviving and progressing in the workplace cannot be an ultimate goal, it is just a stage, a stepping stone. What you need is a life goal, your dream.

Once you have a dream, you know where you are heading and nothing will stop you.

2.2
Having personal values

Every day I am dismayed by the number of people who don't say "Hello", "Please" or "Thank you". Not forgetting those who also try to jump the queue, interrupt you, jostle you, try to steal your work, lie, discriminate, humiliate...

But experience has shown me that, in general, respect attracts respect in return, and kindness begets kindness. To receive, you must know how to give.

This doesn't mean you should let yourself be pushed around or let people walk all over you. Respect isn't submission. By definition the submissive are not respected. You will be respected if you are a good professional, with strong personal values such as justice and empathy, and are endowed with a solid disposition. If your behaviour is poor, you won't be respected. If you feel respected despite your poor behaviour, then it is probably superficial respect. If you are unfair, you will be hated. If you don't have any empathy, you will be seen as a dispassionate machine, soulless. Without a solid disposition, you will be perceived as weak and, consequently, as prey, as a potential and easy victim.

Kindness is just the lack of desire to harm another for the unique pleasure of doing harm. Every company or other human organization has some people who spend their time – and other people's – systematically criticizing, denigrating, mocking and excluding others. Such people are often failures both as professionals and as human beings. Avoid such people as much as possible, but keep an eye on them because they could cause you trouble...

You, on the other hand, should be involved in a process of improvement, construction and collective well-being. Don't criticize. Instead improve the situation, even if it is extremely time-consuming and seems to be a never-ending task. Don't denigrate or mock people, instead help them, encourage them and teach them. Don't exclude, but instead bring people together.

I am reminded of an employee who was his department's favourite punch-bag. He was shy and withdrawn. He didn't share his other colleague's interests and never had a snappy reply to their jokes (which weren't always in good taste). The quality of his work came in for criticism, but I personally always found him to be professional, responsive and competent. One day when I arrived in his department I could hear the others making fun of him. I went to see him, claiming we had an ongoing project, and thanked him for his work and effort so loudly everybody could hear. He told me he appreciated my thoughtful gesture because not many people shared my opinion. But it wasn't an opinion. I was just being factual because he was a conscientious colleague. I also told him – loud enough for the others to hear – that I would personally send an email to his managers to ensure that they were aware of the facts. A prolonged silence descended over the department as I left. I sent my email to his immediate superior, who was also harsh with him, and to his superior's superior and the guy above him. I insisted on the fact that I appreciated this colleague's work and commitment, that the company needed more people like him, and that I hoped his work and commitment would be fairly rewarded in the next annual report. Nobody ever teased him again.

Kindness in the workplace requires you to be impartial while you are working. Regardless of your beliefs and opinions, you should refrain from any kind of discrimination. You aren't dealing with someone of the opposite sex, you aren't dealing with a believer or a non-believer, you aren't dealing with somebody of another colour or from another country. No, you are dealing with a company colleague and a professional. Discriminate only according to ability.

Avoid what's known as "positive discrimination" too, because that's still discrimination. And like all discrimination, it will favour someone to the detriment of another. Why appoint women to an efficient and effective committee for no other reason than it is made up entirely of men? The risk is that something that is working well starts working less well. Similarly, why appoint men to a committee composed entirely of women when it works very well as it is? Why favour the young over the not so young? Maintain your professionalism and ignore the passing trends.

To receive you must first give. It is one of the basic principles of business. If you want the advice of a good professional, it is going to cost you money but you will soon see it not as a cost but as an investment. I discovered this essential truth a long time ago when I called upon the expertise of a chartered accountant to go over my income-tax return. Back then, my salary was a modest one and the expense of several hundred dollars was a big sum for me. But thanks to this chartered accountant, I saved several thousand dollars on my income-tax return. This might seem obvious for many people but for me it was a revelation. I realized that paying for competence wasn't an expense but rather a profitable investment.

Giving is also about giving recognition. We all need to feel alive and appreciated. Every day I see people who look like ghosts. There they are, working among us, but nobody seems to notice them. If our office is clean, it is thanks to them. If our office is protected, it is thanks to them. If the electricity or IT network is working, it is thanks to them. And yet so many people never say to them "Hello" or "Goodbye", not even a "Thank you". Yes, you've guessed it, I'm talking about the cleaners, the receptionists, the security guards and all those other employees who facilitate our daily lives, often for a meagre salary and very little gratitude. I never fail to greet security guards and receptionists in the morning, and salute the cleaning team at the end of the day. I notice that my colleagues who used to ignore them, now acknowledge their existence. Acknowledgement is fundamental to any meaningful interaction. One day you might need this lowly worker whom you despised because he didn't have a job like yours, and wasn't in a position to promote you or make you redundant. The most surprising thing is that lowly worker, whom you probably wouldn't help, will certainly help you when the time comes.

Take constant care of your integrity and your ethics, your reputation is at stake. Not to mention the fact that it is very pleasant to be able to look at oneself with pride in the mirror every morning. Never promise anything you cannot deliver. If you cannot guarantee the result, promise only that you will make the greatest effort and then do your best.

Don't lie even if it is tempting or expedient to do so, or if you are concerned you might get into trouble. Your reputation will be considerably diminished and you will be perceived as an unreliable, even dangerous individual. If you try to cover up a problem, you will probably feel more secure in the short term, but the problem risks coming back at you with interest. The best thing to do is to come clean about the problem swiftly, in clear and factual terms, and put forward concrete solutions that you are ready to implement. You will probably avoid a dressing down, and you will get the chance to show your professionalism, your ability to manage difficult situations, and score points instead of losing face. Once again, be opportunistic and don't forget that problems are almost always opportunities.

But let's not turn this book into an ethics manual. Just try your best to treat others in the way you would like to be treated. And don't forget to be prudent because, even if you have strong personal values, it in no way guarantees that those around you will share those values. Some will even try to take advantage of you, but we'll see later in this book how to avoid falling into some of the more frequent traps.

2.3
Having a solid mindset

If you are to survive, and especially if you are to progress, you will need to take the blows in your stride. It is unavoidable. But with a good mindset, clear principles and goals, and polished skills, you will be able to sidestep most of the blows and those that you do take on the chin will be less painful.

Mindset is conditioned to a great extent by your personal goals and values. Having a goal and strong values will make you strong. Working for a cause that you judge to be greater than yourself, such as an ideal or the well-being of your family, will amplify your inner strength.

What's more, having a good mindset is going to amplify your motivation and your performance within the company. I've tried to identify several key components of the mindset which has energized me and enabled me to succeed. I haven't sorted these components into any kind of hierarchy because, even if some appear to be more important than others, they are part of a whole and I would never have succeeded if one of them had been missing.

The first component is to be able to keep a cool head and rely on your reason more than your emotions. I admit that it is easier to say than do. I've stopped counting the number of times I've replied too quickly or allowed my emotions to colour the tone of an email. Almost immediately I've regretted it, sometimes bitterly. I've also stopped counting all the asinine answers I've given to intelligent questions, thinking I was being quick and clever whereas I was in fact rushing blindly in.

Any biologist will agree, we are all mammals. The human brain may have developed, but it still includes its reptilian features. Every single one of us has the reptilian brain in our head. And every single one of us has natural instincts which, in the modern environment, manifest themselves as fear, desire and joy. The only way I have found to dominate, at least partially, my emotions in the office is to objectify my work as much as possible.

By that I mean being able to demonstrate why I say this, why I recommend that, and why I reject something else. To do this, you need first of all to use logical reasoning founded on realistic and prudent hypotheses, and the available options, and identify the weak points which could attract criticism. Next, your sources of information must be meticulously researched. Thereafter you can explain, using clear reasoning and well-researched data, how you obtained the given result. Only at the very last stage do I let my emotions confirm or cast doubt over this result. If my emotions are comfortable with this objective result, so much the better. If this isn't the case, I go back over it, re-assess my reasoning, perhaps solicit a second opinion, maybe more.

This process has taught me how to take calculated risks. How many people think they've arrived at the right decision by simply following the sheep herd? You only need to look around you. How many people approve a decision without having studied the issue beforehand? How many people give their opinion on studies, books and even films that they have never ever seen? How many rush to buy shares when the truth is it is too late and the stock market crash is imminent? Emotions are powerful and the temptation to follow the herd blindly (or perhaps not) to the abattoir is difficult to overcome. Some might say that it is better being wrong along with everyone else than being right but isolated. In some cases this is true but in others, it is a totally foolish position to take.

Risk-taking is essential to achieving success. Those who never take a risk generally get nowhere, or at best not very far. Compare people who put all their money into savings accounts to those who make well-managed investments. The former earn peanuts in the form of interest and see their savings nibbled away by inflation. The latter fare much better, earning at least 10% a year and secure their gains before the market crashes. But for many, taking a risk means being irresponsible and reckless.

After all, don't we say something like "that's risky" to discourage someone from taking a particular course of action?

When a profitable opportunity presents itself and we look objectively at the obstacles and the potential losses, we are making a preliminary risk analysis. What can we do next to minimize the risks? Start by reading up on the subject and consulting recognized professionals. You will learn more about it and discover that, by taking the right approach, many risks can be reduced and swept aside.

In 2013 I was offered a great job at three times the salary I was then earning. I didn't really know the sector and I lacked some of the necessary skills. But I could easily do about 80% of the work.

My options were simple. I could continue in the relative comfort of my current job, but struggle to repay the mortgage and save for my retirement. Or I could resign and risk being let go at the end of my trial period or not being good enough, but potentially earning triple my salary. My mortgage would be paid off in ten years instead of thirty thanks to a considerable contribution. I could enjoy myself more each month and save a large sum of money. So I bought books on the business sector I was entering, I strengthened my technical knowledge of certain fields, and I spent time with the managers of my new company so I could understand their profession. Within six months I had made up for the problematic 20% of missing skills, at a cost of some long – very long – days at work. But I never regretted my decision and it confirmed two things: staying in your comfort zone is not a profitable option, and learning is an excellent way of overcoming your fears, in particular your fear of taking a risk.

Fear of risk-taking, fear of failure, fear of doing badly holds all of us back. Fear of doing badly and the consequent punishment. The schoolchild who does badly is punished. For how many years, starting in childhood, have we been punished for our mistakes? Mistake equals punishment. Sometimes a punishment is unjustified. I can remember a mathematics exercise that I managed to solve using another method. My method and the result were right, but the teacher marked my paper with a zero. In modern languages I have experienced the situation numerous times where the word I used in English (my native tongue is French) was considered wrong by the teacher. Despite the dictionary backing me up, the situation didn't change because the word was American English and not British English... The same thing happens in French when Belgian or Canadian French is used instead of the French heard in Paris. During an exam, when you ask your neighbour for help or even a sheet of paper because you've run short, you will be punished for cheating.

In business, and thus the workplace, things are different. You need to know how to take (calculated) risks, adapt to situations, and work in a team. If the method is good, then it is very likely the result will be too, and everyone benefits! It is the total opposite of school.

Overcoming your fear is difficult in the face of such conditioning. Even more so when mistakes and differences can be punishable at home too. Learning how to try, to have a go, to dare, to take a calculated risk requires working on yourself, and it is a long and painful road. Some people need to have several successes under their belt before they get the idea, and many more successes before it becomes a natural reflex.

Overcoming one's fear and taking calculated risks often involve unlearning at the same time as learning. We feel fear because we don't know what's going to happen. What's the sole remedy for ignorance? Education. Educate yourself so that you understand the best you can what you didn't know. A plethora of resources is available to help us learn. Multiply your sources of knowledge and points of view on a given subject, identify the weak and strong points, the associated risks and opportunities, listen to the feedback...

At the same time, unlearn what keeps the fear in you alive. Instead of listening to those who want to discourage you, start learning about the subject so you can understand it for yourself. Put some distance between yourself and those friends who try to discourage you. They aren't your friends. A real friend would encourage you, even help you to learn. Keep your distance from all those self-proclaimed experts who give advice but who have never done anything themselves. Thirty peaceful years spent reading the paper in the records office of a bank is sufficient for you to claim, without lying, that you possess thirty years' experience in banking and finance.

Unlearn the second-hand truths and expressions that, when applied to a wide range of situations, turn out more often than not to be misleading. To sort the wheat from the chaff, just keep your eyes open and use your common sense. "Always see it through to the end" can be good advice in some cases, while in others it can turn out to be absolutely disastrous. For example, it is usually a good idea to see your studies through (unless you are Bill Gates or Mark Zuckerberg) whereas pouring good money into a loss-making company until it goes bust is not so good. People often ask me "Why do you like taking risks?" and in general I reply with either "To earn more" or "So I don't end up like you".

When you hear the fateful phrase "In my experience, that doesn't work", ask the person about their experience. Did they really try? How? Did they succeed or fail? Why? More often than not you will find that they never actually tried what you are proposing to do. You might even find that they have never really tried doing anything at all.

When confronted with "It's too complicated", you only have to agree and suggest that you work together to simplify the issue to better understand it. I was hopeless at physics and chemistry but I do remember two things from those lessons at school. One, when you pour hydrochloric acid onto limestone it makes bubbles. Two, when confronted with a complex problem, you need to divide it into a number of simple problems and solve these one by one. I have never managed to apply this principle to physics, but each time I've applied it in my daily life or in a professional capacity, it has always worked. Now imagine a complicated problem in the workplace, one that could make great savings or huge profits if only a solution could be found. And imagine for a moment that you are the one to crack the problem. Imagine how you would benefit in terms of recognition, credibility, annual appraisal, bonus and promotion. Imagine now that you don't do a thing. What would happen? Lastly, imagine that you try to solve the problem? How would you go about it?

When confronted with my dreams and desires, I realized that I never got anywhere when I said to myself "It's too complicated" or "I can't do it". In fact, I was such a bad case that I would often say both at the same time. But one day that all changed when, confronted with my dreams and desires, I thought to myself, "How can I achieve this?" That simple change suddenly allowed me to accomplish many things and achieve almost all my goals, one by one, some rapidly, others slowly, some very slowly. But one thing is certain, I have achieved most of my dreams and desires or am on my way to achieving them. This is because I now ask myself the right question, transform my complex goals and problems into a succession of simple intermediate goals and problems that I can then resolve one by one. I have applied this approach to both my private and professional lives.

I also used to like "That isn't for me" which I've now turned into "Would I like that?" or perhaps "What would I get out of it?" If I like the idea and the game is worth the candle, then "That isn't for me" becomes "I'm in!"

I love excuses like "I don't have time" or "I've got other things to do". Such expressions are only sincerely said in about 1% of cases, the rest of the time they are just a way of legitimizing inactivity. I don't have time for something that earns me more money, but I do have time for lazing in bed watching a TV series. I've got time to be bored and look for things to kill time when I could be looking to learn something that might earn me more money. I was a connoisseur of these kinds of excuses and the benefits they bring: nothing. If something is worth doing and I really don't have the time, I think about how I can find the time. What can I do? What can I stop doing? Who can I stop seeing? If I've got other things to do, I list them in order of potential gains.

I have also learnt that hard work is useless or at best, has little use. For years I worked as hard as a packhorse, almost every day, and didn't count the hours I put in. For years I thought my bosses would appreciate the effort I put in. And they did, and they all thanked me for my time and my personal investment in the job. But none gave me a raise, none promoted me. After a certain number of years (sometimes I'm a little slow on the uptake), the scales fell from my eyes. Some people who did a lot less than me were being promoted, getting bonuses and enjoying generous raises. How was this possible? Everybody always said to me that good things come to those who work hard. And then I discovered that this universal truth didn't apply to me.

It was a huge let-down because I'd been slavishly adhering to the "work hard to make it" ethic and ended up getting nowhere. I worked hard but not intelligently enough, and I hadn't yet learnt 10% of the lessons I am now sharing with you through this book. Today I accomplish the work required of me in my contract, but I very rarely work on weekends, usually leave the office by 6 p.m., and only work 12–14 hour days on average twice a month at the most. And I earn seventeen times my initial salary, the one I earned when I worked like a packhorse.

I also noticed that working for a greater good (greater than oneself) amplified my motivation. Those that, for example, defend an ideal or a meaningful personal project, or who do God's bidding or the nation's work, find in themselves the source of an impressive energy: faith. Faith pushes individuals to move beyond themselves, granting them a steely motivation which increases the range of their actions and thus their capacity to generate results. Faith gives meaning to our actions, our lives. It allows us to be or, at the very least, feel useful.

I've often noticed that those who have faith look for a common interest and sometimes the common interest. The common interest can be wide reaching when faith draws on a religion or a political, patriotic or societal ideal; however the common interest can also be more limited when faith focuses on a family, a project (scientific, artistic, humanist, cultural, etc.) or a group of people.

Being good at your work and creating value for your company are both qualities which, of course, contribute to your survival and progression in the workplace. But you also contribute to the survival and progression of all the people around you. Like you, they probably depend on their company and its good financial health is essential. Essential for funding their accommodation, healthcare and children's education, but also for funding what makes you and your loved ones happy.

And even if you have no faith at all, the efforts you make to survive and progress will gradually lead you to contribute not only to the health of the company, that artificial person in the legal sense of the term, but also to all the people around you. You will be working for yourself, but also for the group of people of which you are a part. Your actions will have an impact which extends beyond you as an individual. Your actions will contribute to your family and loved ones, as well as all those who work with you and, by extension, their families too. You will become ever more useful to the common interest and, in return, you will gain consideration, respect and protection from all those who find you useful.

This process takes time. If you combine it with one or several other factors that stimulate your faith, you will develop a rock-solid mindset which will propel you beyond any limits you might have previously imagined for yourself.

Contributing to the search for the common interest will help you unite people around you and, little by little, you will feel less alone and instead supported by a team which will increase your chances of success. These team-mates, as well as the followers that you manage to win over, will no longer be potential enemies and, as a consequence, you will come up against fewer obstacles. What's more, any potential enemy would think twice, nay thrice before taking you on for fear of having to tackle not just an isolated individual but an entire group of people.

Another fundamental factor in the development of a winning mindset is to not stay on the defensive but start doing.

Shooting a clay pigeon is much easier than taking aim at a real live, healthy pigeon as it flies through the air. If the rifle is a fair shot, the former has practically no chance of dodging the bullet. As for the latter, its chances of survival are much better. It is the same thing in the workplace.

Inactivity gives rise to three distinct risks.

The first acts like coastal erosion, nibbling away at your knowledge, motivation and ability to progress, and risks reshaping you into a millstone around the company's metaphorical neck. You become a target. I will always remember one of my early internships in a company whose accountant refused to use a computer, preferring instead pencil and paper. While a company is in good financial health, making money and tolerant of its employees' quirks, the Luddite has little to worry about. However, when the same company starts to make losses and has to think about cutting costs and restructuring, he or she has just punched their ticket for the next departure. Their chances of survival have reduced to almost nil. As for their chances of progressing, they can forget about that.

The second risk resides in the fact that you are not alone and have rivals. I am reminded of a senior financial officer who was competent but rested heavily on his past glories. He judged himself to be very competent (and he was), that he didn't need to learn and develop and that, without him, the company's costs would not be so well controlled. In reaction to the loss of a large part of the market, the company reorganized itself and he was replaced by a young financial officer who was less competent but cheaper. Certainly he was less experienced, but he did the job sufficiently well for him to retain his position. There was also an experienced engineer I once knew who lost his job when it was delocalized from Paris to Tunisia. The Tunisian engineer did his job just a well but for a significantly lower cost.

Both the senior financial officer and the engineer were overtaken by the competition, one by a younger rival, the other by an international challenger. However one thing I noticed was the managers who did the reorganizing held onto their jobs and got bonuses as a reward for the savings achieved.

The third and final risk regards the often-rapid development of fashions, technologies and techniques. In the 1980s and 1990s, industrial groups such as Xerox, Atari, Amstrad, Compaq and Olivetti were the stars of the computer business. Today, young people have limited knowledge of these brands because some have either disappeared or now focus on other segments which might be less visible to the public. Today, the stars are Google, Facebook, Apple and Amazon. And in twenty years' time, who will be the stars?

In the 1990s who would have imagined that, for example, the giants Nokia, Alcatel and Motorola who then dominated the mobile phone market would cede their hegemony to Samsung, Huawei, Apple and Xiaomi?

Technologies and techniques evolve, professions too. Many of the current professions didn't exist fifty years ago. In 1990 there were no website designers, no content managers and no YouTubers. In twenty years' time the rise of artificial intelligence will threaten a raft of repetitive jobs, even the skilled ones, and new professions will emerge.

How many countries which once experienced a heady boom are now suffering economic difficulties? Does anybody talk of the Asian Tiger economies today? What about the booms in Argentina or Mexico?

And of course fashions change. You just have to watch a film made in 1990, another from 1980 and yet another from 1970 to see the differences.

Being inactive in a world undergoing constant change is to be static in a dynamic environment. In our lives we have had to contend with many changes, some of them radical ones.

Failing to keep up with the times, changes in your profession and developments in your field of business is a dangerous strategy. It is like driving in a straight line. It can work if you are in the desert, but on any tarmac road you'll end up wrapped around a tree at the first bend. Also, you need to anticipate those bends so you can negotiate them smoothly, and there's nothing like learning to help you adapt. Forge ahead continuously by learning continuously.

Doing is a powerful ally which, over time, needs to graft itself on to your DNA.

Doing is the best way to overcome your fear. Are you fearful because of something you don't understand? Well, learn about it. Are you fearful because you think too much? Well stop thinking too much and start doing. And while you are in the heat of the action, you won't have time for metaphysical reflections.

Doing allows you to move forward.

Doing subdues your enemies. If you are doing something, nobody can criticize you for not doing anything. If you are a man or woman of action, you won't be on the defensive all the time. Being on the defensive should be an exceptional position, otherwise you will attract more attacks and, over time, become a first-rate target. Somebody who is a doer will know how to mount an offensive and in the case of an attack, they will know how to execute a robust counter-attack. The assailant will most likely choose another target. It is easier to take on a gentle poodle that likes to doze on the sofa than a spirited German shepherd dog.

Doing is your best ally. It will push you to progress and learn. You will inevitably raise your limits. You will gain an advantage over the competition, whoever they are. Your successes will bolster your confidence in your abilities. You will learn from your mistakes so that next time you will do even better.

As for inaction, that will most certainly cause your ruin. Just sit back and wait for the passage of time to seal your fate.

The fear of doing is tantamount to fearing your best ally to the benefit of an enemy that is as formidable as it is effective: the state of inaction.

Here follows a summary of the key lessons drawn from my personal success which I have mentioned so far and which, it is hoped, will help you develop a solid mindset:

– Be kind.
– Think with your brain, not with your emotions.
– Know how to take risks, which means taking calculated risks.
– Overcome your fear by analysing the facts objectively, by learning and by taking action.
– Learn continuously. Never stop learning.
– Learn how to unlearn and question your beliefs and second-hand ideas. In short, learn how to challenge yourself.
– Avoid people who are negative, toxic and hold you back.
– Be wary of appearances, in particular experts and those that claim to be.
– Stop thinking "I can't do it". Indeed, ban yourself from thinking "I can't do it". From now on, think "How can I do it?"
– Stop working hard and start working intelligently.
– Be opportunistic in the noble sense of the word.
– Set yourself projects and dreams to be achieved, have faith, and concern yourself with the common interest. You'll no longer be chugging along, but firing on all cylinders!
– Take action and don't let inaction destroy you drip by drip. Refuse to let the competition, fashions, techniques and technologies put you out of the game. Gain the upper hand!

Before moving on to the next chapter, there's one more point I would like to add: don't forget your origins.

Regardless of whether you come from a family of workers, aristocrats, shopkeepers or whatever, never forget your origins because they are not only your roots, your identity, but also your starting point, your reference.

You can stagnate at your starting point and never achieve anything in particular. You can regress, go backwards and destroy part of what your ancestors built. Or you can progress and add to what they built. This means consolidating, developing and capitalizing.

While I grew up in the cosy comfort of the middle classes, a pleasant and kindly family environment where my parents always encouraged me and never forced me, my origins are nevertheless modest.

I suffered greatly from the loss of my grandmother who succumbed to Alzheimer's disease. She was born into a good family. She lost her father, the family's only source of income, during the Allied bombings of Paris on a Christmas Eve. She needed to find work quickly and embarked upon a long career as a modest employee in the insurance business. My grandfather, whom she married when he returned from five years' captivity in Germany, did similar work. Both of them worked hard and did their best to put money aside every month. They always made sure I lacked for nothing, even spoiling me somewhat. In her final moments of lucidity, my grandmother suffered the worry of seeing me unemployed and going through divorce. By the time I had turned things around and had started to succeed, she could no longer understand what I said to her. I would have loved to have shown her my success, much of it thanks to her efforts, so that she could have been proud of her grandson.

When she passed away, she left behind a small inheritance. The savings of a lifetime. Worth less than one month of my current salary. That marked me and will stay with me until my dying day. I know where I come from. I know the value of money. I know that what I have managed to build and earn can be easily lost.

Knowing where you come from, comparing what you have built to what your parents achieved, appreciating the value of things and transmitting it to future generations is fundamental to your development. I have seen too many people intoxicated by money, power and glory to the point that they lose sight of the value of things, forget what the love of their own kind feels like, renounce their origins and fabricate a glorious past. They do all this and then implode financially, socially and morally.

Never forget, then, your origins. You will make your parents and grandparents proud. Your children will be proud of their parents and praise your qualities in the playground.

2.4
Having skills and acquiring new ones

To maximize your chances of survival and progression in the workplace, you need to be competent in your field. In other words, you need to be good at your job. And much more.

In the first instance, it means that you should master – or at the very least understand – every aspect of your profession and those of your colleagues. Even if they aren't a specialist in cooking pastries and sauces, the head chef usually knows how to make a cake or a béchamel.

What you haven't mastered will more often than not slip under your radar and you won't even be aware of it. Your boss is likely to ask you questions that you won't be able to answer and you won't have the slightest opinion to offer because your ignorance of the subject prevents you. A negligent, incompetent and lazy colleague can place your project in danger if, through a lack of the necessary knowledge, you aren't capable of reviewing, questioning and checking the quality of their work.

I've seen managers made redundant during company reorganizations because their subordinates were capable of doing the top job just as well, often better, and for less money. On the other hand, I have known managers who could do the work of several subordinates and they weren't laid off, while those under them were.

Don't ignore the next generation because if you stagnate, their skills will catch up with yours and your performance-to-cost ratio won't be so competitive. And don't ignore changing fashions, technical innovations, and international competition which sometimes emanates from countries you wouldn't be able to find on a map.

Stay on the alert for your ego and for common assumptions. "They're late", "They'll never manage it", "We're better than them" and many similar phrases are certainly reassuring but they also lull you into a false sense of security. Xerox salesmen were considered to be part of the business elite. And they were, but what do you sell when the print and photocopy market disappears under the weight of 100% digitization? Then there's Nokia, once the leading mobile phone manufacturer, where are they now in the sales rankings? And what about the Russians and how they trailed the Americans in developing the atomic bomb? It didn't prevent them from catching up in the space of just a few years. Today China is home to some of the largest companies on the planet, is preparing to send astronauts to the moon, and is a leader in the field of artificial intelligence. And yet a mere thirty years ago nobody would have believed you if you told them this was going to happen.

Never rest upon your laurels. You might no longer be hungry, but others are famished and salivating at the prospect of getting their hands on your dinner. Sometimes your rivals are a few metres away, sometimes thousands of kilometres distant, sometimes both.

It is imperative that you strengthen your skills and broaden their scope.

If you work in support, you need to learn about the practical realities of your company's business. How many specialists in quality assurance, auditing, steering, procurement, finance, human resources and so on work at head office and have absolutely no connection with the people in the field? How many truly understand how their company's products or services are designed, produced and marketed?

Such disconnection from the base results in work not being done to support the company, but to maintain instead layers of administrative complexity which can weigh heavily on the company's financial performance. Once again, what is considered a problem or an inevitability for the majority should be seen by you as an opportunity.

Let's take the example of returned and unsold items. Both cost companies dearly, sometimes very dearly, year in year out. Companies often generate statistics using sophisticated computer applications that crunch and consolidate data supplied in a rush by underpaid and overworked operators to produce fancy 3D graphs. Analysts with the right qualifications analyse the data and turn it into fabulous reports for their management. More often than not, none of them ever had to deal with a customer. Why isn't the product selling? Why is the product getting sent back? Analysts should spend more time at the sales outlets and the warehouses managing the returns to understand the real causes of the situation and to discuss practical solutions with the sales force, the logistics team and even the customers themselves.

I don't know of any director who would say "No" to the following speech: "Unsold items have increased X% on last year and returns are up Y%, resulting in an annual cost of Z million dollars for the company. We've crunched the numbers but we need to understand the real causes so we can implement the best remedial measures. I propose to spend three months in our various sales outlets to observe and analyse the problem of unsold items with our sales force and the issue of returns with our logistics teams, and then come back to you with a comprehensive report, including a costed action plan, put together in collaboration with representatives of the finance, sales and logistics departments. All I need is your green light..." These kinds of initiatives will transform you from a lowly analyst into a provider of solutions, a consolidator, a leader. It is an opportunity for you to get yourself noticed in the upper echelons and to progress.

Nevertheless you need to understand your products (ideally by trying them daily), learn how the logistics work, get familiar with customer behaviour, draw lessons from the market sector, discover what influences rises and falls in demand... In short, you need to learn a lot. Immerse yourself in books, the internet, available reports, competitors' websites, and blogs written by testers and other professionals. Go out of your way to meet the sales and logistics professionals in your company, and explain to them that you are trying to understand the current situation. Take them out to lunch if necessary. The investment will be worth it. You'll learn. What's more, you will establish useful contacts for the future who can, when the time comes, be organized into a team that can assist you.

By working in this way you will learn a maximum of new information, strengthen your skills and create opportunities for scoring points with your hierarchy.

You also need to learn how the people above you and below you in the company operate.

Managers report to the directors who in turn report to shareholders. Most shareholders want to hear just one word: profit. In other words, deliver added value to a manager or a director and you'll help them obtain the approval of their superiors. They too want to survive. They too want to progress.

If two of your largest competitors merge, there's a big chance they will become even more dangerous. To stand a chance, your company will have to be even more productive. The issues of missed sales opportunities and the waste generated by having to manage returns will become even more critical and pressing. Once again, this is good for you.

Compare the profitability of your company and that of your competitors. If your company isn't doing so well, the directors are probably under pressure from the shareholders to do better. Any solution is going to be welcomed with open arms. Get working on it!

When it comes to returned items, you will almost certainly have to deal with warehouse staff. Understand their job and how it has changed over time. What was it like when they joined the company? They will probably tell you that there were ten more people in the team five years ago, that the workload has gone through the roof in the last three years, that bright young consultants turned up in their fancy suits to set up a stock reporting tool which wastes everyone's time...

You might discover that the stock reports are unreliable, that boxes in the app are ticked at random, and that the management is completely unaware of the real state of affairs.

Perhaps a simpler computer tool and regular contact with the warehouse staff would solve the problem. Create your own network from your level in the company down to the field operators. You will learn about what is going on in the real world, enjoy a special connection with the field staff, and put an extra lap or two of the race between you and your colleagues who can't be bothered to do the same. Obtain the information you need, but also improve the lot of the warehouse staff. For example, you could save them time by reducing the quantity of information they have to key into the IT system. Note down the figures, and replace the tick boxes with regular discussions in the flesh. It is a win-win for everyone. You and your management will have reliable data; the warehouse staff will have an easier job.

Don't just learn about the technical side.

Learn about communication too. Make your messages powerful. Learn to sell, to convince, to present something complex in a simple way. Learn how to use a presentation program like Microsoft PowerPoint and become an expert in it. Learn the basics of rhetoric to help you fend off attacks from your opponents.

Learn the basics of law if you are a technician, engineer or in finance. If you are an engineer or a lawyer, learn the basics of finance, and know how to read a balance sheet and a profit and loss statement.

Learn the basics of economics. Take an interest in geopolitics.

Learn about yourself and learn how to look objectively at your life. Learn from the lives of others and their experiences. Read biographies on people who arouse your curiosity. Learn about the history of companies, countries and cultures. Take an interest in philosophy and discover or rediscover the writings of the Stoics. In particular, read or re-read Marcus Aurelius and his famous work Meditations.

Learn about science, the universe and the animal kingdom. Animals have much to teach us about ourselves.

Explore works of science fiction to help you see into the future.

Books, the internet, radio, conferences, newspapers, podcasts: take advantage of the abundance of media available today.

Understand the world you are living in, the circles you are moving in, the sector you are working in, and the people you frequent, the profession you practise, the rivals you pose a threat to, and ultimately yourself.

Learn. More and more. And above all, never stop learning.

Failure very often proffers the excuse that it didn't have time to learn, that age wasn't on its side, or that school was a long time ago. And yet every successful person that I have ever known was filled with an insatiable desire to learn. They educate themselves willingly so that they can achieve the various stages of their goals. Just read the biographies or the writings of history's great leaders, or those who are achieving success in the world today, and you will see that they all share a thirst for knowledge and understanding.

If you want to learn, surround yourself with successful people. Learn from them. Learn from the best. They will pull you up, not drag you down. If you don't know any, read the books they write, watch their videos or interviews, sign up for their training courses, listen to their podcasts... There are plenty to choose from, especially today.

If you are not much of a reader, don't worry. Set yourself the goal of reading twenty pages a day, which is ten actual sheets of paper a day and, in fact, very little. But over a single month, that makes 600 pages, which is easily two books! Over twelve months, that makes twenty-four books, and 120 books in the space of five years. It is an enormous goal yet so easily attained. Just a little effort every day, maintained over time, and you'll get there.

2.5
Having an open mind and a broad perspective (nexialism)

A narrow mind or a limited perspective will reduce your chances of survival in the workplace and eliminate almost any chance of progress.

Like a car driver, the danger can be ahead of you, behind you, on either side of you, or in your blind spots. And also like a car driver, knowing the area, the shortcuts and the busy periods will help you save time.

Remember the key points of the previous chapters: never stop learning, nothing is illogical, be kind. Observing these three precepts will help you broaden your perspective exponentially, help you sidestep most of the dangers in your path, and help you detect a significant number of opportunities.

Many people are satisfied with simply contemplating what they see. A small minority seek to understand how it came about. And an even smaller minority – not to say a tiny minority – seek to understand not only how it happened but also why. This is a no-brainer. If you want to increase your chances of surviving and progressing in the workplace, you should be a member of that tiny minority.

First, develop the habit of multiplying perspectives. In the case of a disagreement between several people, take the time to understand the fears and aspirations behind the demands of each person involved. And understand why.

I am reminded of a confrontation between employees of a production site and their management. The employees wanted higher wages. The management on the other hand explained that this wasn't possible because of the poor financial results. From that moment onwards they engaged in a particularly tumultuous dialogue without really listening to each other.

How do you resolve a problem like that? By increasing wages, obviously, because that is what the employees wanted. Indeed, despite the poor financial results, a small rise could have been brought to the table without endangering the company's survival. But after digging a little deeper, by talking to the employees on the periphery, I realized that they were suffering on the factory floor. The pace of the work was too fast. Automation which made the work relentless and noisy, compounded by years of doing the same repetitive movements, was simply wearing them out physically and mentally. Exacerbated in no little way by the almost inhuman rigidity of certain foremen who would even refuse a worried mother time off to go and see her child in the hospital.

The nub of the problem wasn't money, then, but the exhausting working conditions and the lack of consideration. Slowing down the pace of production was compensated by reorganizing shifts. Breaks were extended and break rooms made cosier. Refreshments such as tea, coffee and fresh fruit were made available in a calmer environment which also featured comfortable, relaxing chairs for people to enjoy. Breads and pastries were made available each morning and employees left an hour earlier on Fridays. The additional cost was a drop in the ocean for the management. The atmosphere on the factory floor improved noticeably and the employees appreciated the efforts made.

The company continued to suffer financial difficulties for another two years, but didn't have to deal with a single demand to raise wages in that time. The third year turned out to be much more profitable. Each employee was awarded a bonus equal to one month's salary without even asking for it. Not a single employee resigned from the company in that period.

Wage demands are often the monetization of a deeper malaise. Employees would certainly grumble less if, in certain countries, the taxes they pay guaranteed a decent retirement, protection from unemployment, good policing, effective healthcare and proper education. The truth of the matter is that such grumblings are, for the most part, justified by the fact that taxes continue to rise, that retirement provision is under threat, that job insecurity is growing, policing decreasing, and the quality and availability of healthcare and education is steadily diminishing. Handing out a few hundred dollars every year is never going to be enough to solve the problem.

Multiplying your perspectives and trying to understand the whys and wherefores are therefore essential precepts. As is the habit of replacing excuse-thoughts such as "This isn't for me" or "I can't do it" with proactive ones like "How can I achieve this?"

History is a precious ally. Endeavour to understand the history of the company that employs you. Seek out someone in the company who has lived through a good part of its history, especially an executive employee. Go to see him or her and explain that you want to learn more about the key events of the company, its DNA, and that you heard they were the best person for this. If they are really busy, try to meet up for lunch. Learn about the culture of the various companies that merged, their strengths, their weaknesses, and find out who came from which company. Get to grips with the differences of opinion, the clans, and the battles fought... Not only will you learn much about your daily work environment but you will have made yourself a high-level contact and your curiosity won't go unnoticed.

In addition to the company annals, delve into the history books. Peruse the history of technology, fashion, religion, philosophy, science and civilization. Learn about the lives of exceptional people. Your mind will gain in lucidity with every reading.

History tends to repeat itself. It will provide you with pertinent analogies to current situations. You can reflect on how a historical outcome might apply to the situation you are experiencing right now. Did sales of similar products collapse twenty years ago? Ask yourself how and why. What mistakes were made and what remedies were applied at the time?

Indeed, the present was forged in the past. Analyse the situation as it was fifty years ago, twenty years ago, ten years ago, five years ago, last year and how it is today. Trends will appear, including rises, falls, cycles and accidents, and you should try to identify them and explain how they came about. Try to project these trends into the future. A person who thinks like this will probably be several moves ahead of the rest, just like a seasoned chess player.

Understand all the points of view, seek out the whys and wherefores, and look to history to help you develop the broadest possible perspective.

Combine these efforts with continuous training in multiple fields which, over time, will end up intersecting to a certain degree. You will develop an exceptional ability to adapt, to anticipate, and to resolve complex problems.

Explore every field of knowledge, even the art of communicating. Learn to cultivate your image, study the fundamentals of psychology, and develop an interest in neuroscience by reading science magazines which interpret complex subjects for the general public. As a result, you will optimize your communication, convey your messages more effectively, and find it easier to sell your ideas.

In his book The Voyage of the Space Beagle, the author Alfred van Vogt gave a name to this ability to connect multiple branches of knowledge. He called it "nexialism".

A manager versed in the art of nexialism is a very effective executive. Their results are unique because he or she leverages a multitude of factors that make their actions precise, targeted, and subject to minimal turbulence.

Keep your mind open and cultivate your nexialism. You will expand your mental and creative abilities and, in the long run, your results.

Over the years I have had to deal with particularly complex insurance claims. Some amounting to tens, even hundreds of millions of dollars. In some cases I was able to increase the indemnity by as much as 50%.

How? By checking and challenging the work of the loss adjuster, line by line. Without any previous formal training I had managed to learn the basics in law, management, logistics, tax, insurance, spreadsheet programs, project management and so on. Knowledge of these fields enabled me to follow the discussions, ask the right questions and subsequently coordinate a group of experts. For every debatable point we put together a counter argument whose technical and legal aspects were robustly demonstrated. And then we proposed an alternative sum. The strategy more than paid off. If I had lacked knowledge of insurance, it wouldn't have worked. If I had lacked knowledge of project management or law, it wouldn't have worked. This strategy did indeed work because, although by no means an expert, I was sufficiently well grounded in these various fields. The added value was considerable.

All the best managers, experts, leaders, and entrepreneurs that I've ever met subscribed to the idea of nexialism and spent an inordinate amount of time learning. Often they almost exclusively associated with people who could teach them new things, who influenced them in a positive way.

2.6
Having the ability to watch and listen

Most of us have the ability to see and hear. And yet very few of us really know how to watch and listen.

When I entered the world of work with my little ego inflated by a recently acquired diploma, I would talk and do but I didn't know how to watch and listen. And that set me up for a lot of disappointment.

In order to understand a problem and detect opportunities, you need to be able to watch and not just see. Which takes us back to the how and why. Watching involves understanding the how. Detailed watching supplemented by the appropriate knowledge will enable you to define the why.

Watching a problem means observing it from when it took root to its fruition. Where did it start? What path did it take? How did it grow? What factors promoted or hindered the growth of the problem? All these elements have to be explored and clarified.

Sometimes a problem isn't just technical in nature. Problems (and therefore opportunities) often inhabit interfaces. An interface between two contractors or departments, an interface coordinating several contracts, interfaces connecting several IT systems or software solutions... The greater the size of the company and its workforce, the greater the number of interfaces. It only needs two people who can't get along, each working in a different department, for files sent by one to end up at the bottom of the pile on the other's desk. Sometimes departments are engaged in fighting a full-blown war.

In meetings, watch who looks at whom and their expressions. You will see secret smiles, winks, worried stares, discreet signals, even discussions via WhatsApp or WeChat...

Listen to everyone's opinions, too. Listen to rumours but treat them with the cautious scepticism they deserve. Never forward them.

Your senses are precious allies. Don't forget that you are walking on risky terrain and that the workplace is the modern equivalent of the jungle. Don't forget that you don't just have a brain and a heart, you have eyes and ears too.

2.7
Having the taste for a job well done

Something done reluctantly will probably be done less well than if it were done willingly.

Your reputation is a key asset and you should take great care of it. It can take years to build, but just a few negligent mistakes can demolish it.

Do tasks that you find to some extent enjoyable and interesting. If not, try to change them if you can.

If you do something you like, your work will be less tiring and done better because it will be a source of satisfaction and motivation. You will naturally get more involved and be more motivated to explore the subject in greater detail, broaden your scope and improve the situation. You will capitalize on your core knowledge, because your expertise will develop with every passing day and increase in scope. In short, if you enjoy your work you will increase your chances of promotion, albeit by perhaps moving to a new company.

2.8
Having the time

Time is your most precious resource. We would all like to have more time, but unfortunately none of us can expand those twenty-fours hours that make up the day.

As we grow older we become more aware that time passes quickly and is a limited resource. We also realize that we spend the greater part of our lives sleeping, working and travelling, including the trip to and from work. We realize that we spend more time at work than at home with our families.

Nevertheless it is up to us to manage this passing time, to waste it or make the most of it.

Concerning sleep, when I was a student I could work or party all night and still go to the university lectures the following day without the slightest problem. Nowadays if I have a night out, it takes me an entire week to recover. So I try as much as possible to limit the number of late nights during the week, only going out on Fridays and Saturdays. I rarely stay out after one o'clock in the morning.

I used to go to bed at all hours of the night and then get up late the next day. One day I read an article about successful people. It said they went to bed at regular times and got up early. I thought it was a joke. How can getting up early contribute to your success? How does going to bed at the same time every night improve your chances of success? I couldn't see the correlation.

Some time later I was required to get to work early every day for a fortnight. Getting up at 5 a.m. was hard, and I was exhausted by about 9 p.m. But after several days of this I realized that my working days had become more productive and I was getting a lot more done. The early morning is peaceful, devoid of hustle and bustle. No telephone calls. No emails. No colleagues knocking on your door. With only the company of a hot cup of coffee, my first working hours of the day allow me to focus very efficiently on the most complex of projects. By adopting this habit of going to bed earlier and rising earlier, and by sticking to it, I feel less tired and generally on better form. And instead of slogging away into the night, I stop and go home earlier.

So the joke was on me, because that article was a revelation and a recipe for efficiency. I now understand the truth in the age-old proverb "the early bird catches the worm".

At work, I also had a number of preconceived hopes and ideas which, in the end, never helped me achieve anything but waste a lot of time.

The first of these beliefs was "work hard to earn more". If this is true, all I have to do is work really hard and I'll earn even more. And if I work my fingers to the bone, surely I'll hit the jackpot. That was the simple, not to say simplistic reasoning knocking around in my head. So I overworked myself for years without counting the hours and even less my weekends. I even replied to every single email when I was on holiday.

At the end of the first year I expected to be rewarded for so much effort but received nothing. At the end of the second year, nothing. Perhaps I needed to be patient and wait for the end of the third year... I was always given glowing reports full of compliments and flattery, but I never got an extra bonus or a promotion. And yet people around me who seemed to be doing half the work I was doing, and leaving the office at 5 p.m. every evening, were getting promoted and received extraordinary bonuses. It just didn't make sense.

And then the fateful day arrived when my health gave out and I ended up in hospital. Thenceforth I could no longer wear myself out like before because my health was at risk. So I had no option but to work less and leave earlier in the day. And I still managed to produce the same results at the end of the year!

In fact, I was being asked to do my job and nothing more. And then I remembered this aphorism attributed to Confucius:

"Whoever exceeds his objective, fails to reach it." He was 200% right with those wise words.

My basic job required me to work no more than a few hours daily to do it well. Suddenly I had a lot of time on my hands. Not only did I leave earlier in the evening and have more time for my personal life, but I also had more time for working on special projects that would enhance my career and salary.

I always take great care over choosing these special projects. No more than three a year. And they must be successful. To achieve this, I focus all my efforts on these three projects and do not spread myself too thinly. In general I announce the two easiest in my goals for the year and undertake the third separately. If it doesn't succeed as planned, I won't be penalized for it at the end of the year. I arrange things so that my workload, including my daily duties and my two or three special projects, remains reasonable and doesn't prevent me from leaving the office early.

I also seek to save time in order to achieve these projects in the best way possible. As I'm not a genius, I like to take inspiration from those that are. A certain Albert Einstein, for instance, set off yet another light bulb in my head. When a journalist asked him what he would do if he only had an hour to solve a life-threatening problem, he replied that he would spend fifty-five minutes understanding the problem and only the last five minutes devising the solution. By applying this principle, I manage to resolve complex situations and achieve most of my special high-value projects.

I park the problem or question in a corner of my mind, and let time work on it. The subject becomes gradually clearer and simpler. Ideas take shape, while the strategy and its attendant actions develop step by step. And after several months gestating the action plan becomes clear, almost fully formed and nearly ready for execution. The time passed on these high-value projects is thus kept to a minimum. Time which I can use to do something else.

The workplace has also taught me not to give without receiving. An illustration of this concept at its most fundamental level is when your boss comes to see you to entrust you with a new project. Without fail, I show (or feign) a lively interest in his or her proposition. If the project has merit, high added value, and has the potential to earn some brownie points with the hierarchy, I agree to look over it for twenty-fours in order to assess whether I have the ability to do it justice. If the project is of no particular interest, apart from adding to my workload, my answer is always the same: "I would very much like to take this on. However I am managing a large number of projects and if I deal with this one, I will have to abandon projects X and Y (i.e. endeavours that will allow my boss and I to impress the hierarchy)." The reply is often the same: "Indeed, keep working on X and Y, they take priority. Somebody else can do this task." And it works. What you need to do is to set the uninteresting task against something that your boss doesn't want to lose or that will cause more problems than he or she already has.

I have learnt to avoid pointless meetings or ones where my presence is not absolutely required by a superior. I always enquire about the subject of the meeting, what is expected of me, what value my presence is expected to add, and so on. If a minor item involving me is on the agenda, I let somebody in my team prepare the subject and, once we have gone over it together, let them present it on my behalf. Yet more hours saved in the week.

Of course, I often just say "No". Anything that is not absolutely essential, does not have the potential for saving or generating money, and has no connection with my goals, I will usually refuse. Usually, because I do sometimes make exceptions, in particular to help a colleague whom I like and who needs my expertise.

And I also refuse to attend a meeting for the meeting's sake. I stay in my office if I have something to accomplish, otherwise I leave. There is no point in hanging your jacket on the back of a chair to give the impression that you are present when everybody knows it is bogus. It is not unknown for me to stay in the office until 10 p.m. but it is very unusual. It only happens on major projects when I can't avoid it, perhaps because of a tight deadline or collaborators working in different time zones.

In addition to better managing my sleep and work, I have also learnt how to manage my personal life better.

First of all, I delegate certain tasks such as the cleaning and the ironing, which saves me one day a week. But I never delegate free time with my children. For example, some parents send their children off to a cookery lesson. In my view it is better to teach your children to cook yourself. They love learning from their parents, you create fond memories and above all you won't regret a thing when they become adults and you realize that you didn't spend enough time with them when they were young. And if you don't know how to cook or haven't tried the recipe before, learn it together. It'll be more fun.

Next, to save time, I avoid useless or negative people. I've stopped socializing. Instead, I prefer spending time with my family, my real friends (those who are there when times are hard, who always encourage me, who give me ideas, and with whom I can talk about anything and everything) and people who teach me new things. Wasting three hours talking about the weather, the traffic or other people, comparing cars or houses, or listening to an inveterate boaster just isn't for me.

And then there is the trip to and from work. By moving closer to my workplace I have saved an hour every day on public transport, which amounts to a hefty five hours a week. In other words half a day saved every week, it is as simple as that. To save even more time, I even take the bus. This astonishes my colleagues who prefer to turn up in their fancy SUVs even though they live even closer to the company offices than me. Not only can you reduce travelling times, you can also use the time in another way. You can relax your mind by looking out of the window, or you can learn something new. You can read in the train if it is a longish trip. In the car, you can listen to a podcast or the radio.

And of course, doing nothing sometimes does your mind and soul the world of good. Often when I'm asked about my plans for the weekend, I just say: "Nothing, I'm going to relax in bed with a novel or watch a good film."

2.9
Having the right friends

Life isn't simple and its duration is limited. We have seen that we can save time, sometimes a great amount, by adhering to certain simple principles.

Of the simple principles you can implement, we have already mentioned the idea of not wasting time on people who are useless, negative or toxic. Not only do such people eat up your time and consequently your life but they also tend to lower your potential and standards. Let's look at some of the common character traits I have noticed about time-wasters.

First, time-wasters teach you nothing except for the fact that they are soon going on holiday to the Maldives or have bought a new car. You might also get to hear the latest gossip or a report on the week's news. Such people like to make you feel that they are somehow better than you, are more successful than you when the truth is often entirely the opposite. Don't waste your time with braggarts and fools who exist only for buying stuff and showing off. Nobody is impressed by a luxury car or a fancy house which has been bought on credit and which, so long as the loan or thirty-year mortgage hasn't been paid off, remains the property of the bank.

In addition to the show-offs, you also need to avoid people you can never trust. Untrustworthy people typically feed off the confessions of their "friends" to kindle the curiosity of their other "friends". You can never be sincere with such people. They turn your misfortunes into stories which will ensure the success of their next dinner party. Your projects will become public knowledge. And sometimes things you have said will be used against you.

Next up are the toxic pessimists. For them, everything is "impossible", your goals are "unachievable", your dreams are just "illusions", and nothing you consider doing is ever "the right thing for you". Such individuals are particularly dangerous because they chip away at your hopes from the very start, and they sow doubts in your mind which can paralyse you and prevent you from taking action.

They often say things like: "This isn't for people like us", "You need money or connections to be able to do that", "You'll never do it", "It's impossible", "Keep your head down", "What will the neighbours say?", "You're taking a big risk", "Ambition is dangerous", "Life isn't just about money", "You should be happy with what you've got", "Look around you, there are many people worse off than you"... The list is long and I could easily devote an entire book to the subject.

And yet, when you look into it, you will find that many successful people started out with little, even nothing. Warren Buffett had a few thousand dollars which he managed to grow into a fortune without relying on any special connections. How can such people, who have often never done anything with their lives other than find excuses for not doing something, know that you won't achieve your goals? Have they at least tried themselves? How can anybody say that something is impossible if they haven't tried? How can anyone say that something is impossible when many others have tried and have actually succeeded?

Yes, it was once impossible to travel from London to Tokyo in a few hours. Yes, it was once impossible to fly to the moon, talk to somebody on the other side of the world from the comfort of your office, graft an artificial heart, study in the best Western universities if your skin was the wrong colour... And yet all these things are now possible.

Avoid the defeatists who keep you tethered to mediocrity, which is in fact their mediocrity. Instead dare to try and have a go, and if you fail, never mind, it will work better the next time. Educate and train yourself to be a contender in the ocean of life and then dive in. You will discover that you aren't out of your depth and that while swimming is hard work, you can strike out into exciting new waters.

Sometimes we can't avoid such people because they are members of our own family and we love them. They seek to dissuade us from attempting something we want to do because they are afraid for us. They are afraid you will fail. If this is the case, change the subject and don't talk about your projects. Instead, appreciate the people you love for their good qualities and try not to trigger their faults.

So who should you be spending time with? People who teach you new things, who inspire you, encourage you and offer you their help unconditionally. Remember, true friends are supportive.

We tend to resemble the people who live and work around us. This is normal. It is part of our nature. Hang out with mediocre people and you will become mediocre. Surround yourself with the best and you will get better yourself.

Many people who were the top of the class at school, in their home town or village, think themselves to be above the average. But once they enter one of the best universities, they soon realize that there are many better than them. Suddenly they are no longer competing with the best from their home town, but rubbing shoulders with the cream of the country and perhaps beyond. And that changes everything. After leading the provincial pack, they are now laggards who have to make up for lost time by pushing themselves to the limit if they are to earn a place on the podium. Some fall by the wayside, while others develop a record-breaking mindset which propels them to the front of the race, perhaps even making them the winner.

Try to learn from the successful by spending time with them. I don't just mean financial success, but success in all its forms. For example, dedicated scientists who discover incredible things will talk enthusiastically about their work, about the best moments of their careers and the difficulties they have faced. They are often brilliant people who are more interested in finding the funds to finance their research than earning a mint to pay for the swimming pool in their garden.

You can learn from politicians when they hold public meetings or by joining a political party. They will tell you about their early days, how they started out, the obstacles they had to overcome, the lessons they have learnt, and how they achieved success. Some will be delighted by the interest you show in their career, so seek them out and learn from them, and don't be content just to hear their false promises while you are waiting for the free buffet at the end of the meeting.

Seek out people who have been successful in business. Even if you can't get to meet Bill Gates, Richard Branson, Elon Musk or Bernard Arnault, you can always read their books and listen to their interviews. There are undoubtedly numerous entrepreneurs around you who have achieved success, perhaps the owner of a major car dealership, a highly regarded restaurateur, or a franchise investor. Some will be close to where you live and you won't have to go far out of your way to meet them.

And then there are all the great men and women who have shaped the history of the world: kings and queens, scientists, genius inventors, philosophers, industrialists, financiers, philanthropists, religious leaders, revolutionary guides, tyrants and benefactors. Numerous books, videos, films and podcasts trace their lives and careers. If you can't meet them, you can always share in the secrets of their successful lives through the accounts and biographies written about them.

This is also a good moment to mention a certain number of bestsellers which are readily available and excellent for developing your mindset, your focus and the foundations of your future success. Prefer the writings of exceptionally successful businessmen – Warren Buffett, Ray Dalio, Robert Kiyosaki, Richard Branson – over works by psychologists, university lecturers or obscure specialists. The very nature of their careers makes them fundamentally interesting and I can but only recommend you read their books, listen to their interviews, watch their videos and download their podcasts. You won't waste your time, on the contrary it will be a veritable investment.

2.10
Having good health

To succeed, you need to be on form. And to do that, you don't have any other choice than to take care of your health and yourself.

As we have seen previously, you need to jettison everything that wastes your time. Use your time to do what you enjoy, educate yourself and relax.

I am not a top-level sportsman, far from it, but I rediscovered what it means to feel good physically thanks to an exceptional sports coach in Geneva.

He was a great coach and helped me through a particularly difficult period. Several deaths in the family, my divorce and a very tense situation at work resulting from the company's reorganization... And my morale was at its lowest. My pleasure at that time involved going home with a pizza to watch a good film. And a vicious circle established itself, eating comfort food to compensate, and the more I put on weight, the more I felt tired and put myself down. And the more I put myself down, the more I ate and the more I shut myself away. I managed to keep abreast of my work because I knew how to do my job well and I kept on top of my tasks. But my personal life had hit rock bottom.

Thanks to a progressive and undemanding programme tailored specifically to me, I managed to lose weight. I didn't need to jump on the bathroom scales to assess my progress because I could feel the heaviness which had paralysed me was gradually dissipating. It was if I was dropping burdensome weights one by one. I felt better. Better physically and better mentally. Of course I had to eat less and better.

I reconnected with my self-confidence, rediscovered my strength and felt ready to once again face the challenges that would inevitably come my way.

Hiring a great coach was one of the best investments I've ever made. Instead of wasting my money on useless things, on uninteresting objects, on restaurant dinners with time-wasters and toxic people, I invested in my health. The return on investment was incredible and I continue to work with a sports coach twice a week.

Being overweight sapped my morale and each time I put on a bit of weight, I felt tired, irritable and put myself down.

Poor health will prevent you from guiding your projects to fruition. You should therefore ensure that you are firing on all cylinders and not stuck in bed. Have regular health checks. Once a year have your teeth checked by a dentist, your eyes by an ophthalmologist, your hearing by an ENT specialist. If you are a woman, have regular check-ups for breast cancer. If you are a man, prostate cancer. Have a look at your health insurance to see if you are eligible for free health check-ups, it is worth it.

If you are feeling tired all the time, having trouble concentrating at work or focusing on the road when you are behind the wheel, you might be suffering from sleep apnoea. Ask your doctor to recommend a specialist and get a diagnosis. If it turns out that you are suffering from sleep apnoea, get treated. It will stimulate your energy, your ability to focus and your performance.

I have also noticed the benefits of walking to and from work every day. The fresh morning air helps you wake up, and the walk gives you time to reflect on how to organize the day's work and tackle urgent tasks. By the time you get to work, you'll be hitting the ground running. Walking home at the end of the day will give you a chance to review the day's work and blow off some of the accumulated steam. If you live too far from your workplace, go for a walk at lunchtime or get off the bus one stop early.

In short, take care of your health. You will enjoy greater stamina and be more efficient, more resilient, and more responsive over time. You will reduce your exposure to injuries and illnesses that could endanger more than just your success in the workplace.

2.11
Having a mentor

Having one or several mentors is a great opportunity, especially at the beginning of your career when you aren't that familiar with the ins and outs of your business. However, while having a mentor is an opportunity to be seized, it can also turn into a risk that could endanger your future. So be prudent.

Most of the time your mentor will be someone higher up in the hierarchy who sees in you potential, perhaps considering you to be a protégé. Your mentor could also be a teacher, a family friend, a member of an association or a professional body... Usually, mentors choose their protégés rather than the other way round, basing their decision on instinct. Many things can attract the eye of a mentor, such as an unusual turn of phrase, an interesting idea, a pertinent point of view, or better than average technical or social skills. Sometimes the mentor will see you as an ideal child or be reminded of their own early days in the job.

Mentors have two precious attributes to share with their protégés.

First, their experience in business and in the company. They can get you quickly up to speed with the idiosyncrasies of your workplace, and introduce you to useful and influential contacts. They can also provide considerable beneficial advice, training and coaching to help you develop the strongest hand at the table.

Next, your mentor will probably want to help you prove your worth to the company by carefully selecting advantageous tasks that they will deliver to you on a plate. In order to foster your success, and indirectly their own, your mentor will certainly mark out the best path to follow and do their best to flag up the pitfalls.

Having a mentor is a major asset. Of course, you can achieve success without the help of a mentor, and there are numerous examples of people doing just that. But having a mentor will help you progress more quickly, and might even allow you to skip certain stages in your development.

If you are indeed lucky enough to have a mentor, bear in mind the potential associated risks.

First off, you might fall into the trap of putting your trust into an incompetent or false mentor.

An incompetent mentor is usually a superficial colleague who will end up wasting your time and might even turn out to be toxic. Some company veterans enjoy giving advice to newcomers. The quality of such advice depends directly on the quality of the adviser. If your mentor has had an honourable career, enjoys a solid reputation in the company, can claim some remarkable achievements and earns a particularly enviable salary, you can safely assume that you are dealing with a credible adviser and one who can contribute value to your career. On the other hand avoid those potential mentors who have been marginalized or shunted off to an unimportant corner of the company, who always have something to say about the management's decisions but never take action, who tell you how to manage your relationships despite having several failed marriages under their belt... As a rule, follow the advice and example of those who have achieved success.

A false mentor will abuse the inexperience and gullibility of the youngest employees to present him or herself as the fount of all knowledge. And yet the truth is they have never created anything, never achieved a goal, never turned their abundant words into real actions. They will pretend to teach you and give you precious advice, and you may well fall for their illusion. So if you don't want to have your time and energy wasted by a false mentor, the first thing to do is check the veracity of their achievements, their successes, their reputation and their familiarity with the upper echelons of the company. If it turns out that you are dealing with a false mentor, remain courteous and respectful, give them some of your time to avoid making an enemy, but nothing more.

Being manipulated by your mentor is also a risk. They can exploit your inexperience, your overflowing energy, your motivation, your gullibility and perhaps even your cupidity so you will do their dirty work and take the risks that they would never dream of taking. If this is the case, be sure to beat a hasty exit. You need to spot manipulators quickly and, even if you are just starting out, put your trust in a very useful friend: your instinct.

In addition to the incompetence, fakery and flakery, another mentor-associated risk that you need to be permanently on the alert for is what I call "The Guru". This is a charismatic person who seeks to manipulate the weak-minded and the unconfident. Unlike a real mentor, a guru will not help you progress and improve and has no interest in your personal and professional development.

You also need to be prudent when it comes to the relationships your mentor maintains within the company. If they are a member of a clan, make sure that doesn't come back to bite you one day. Don't forget that you need to have as much support as you can within the company. Being part of a clan or being associated with one can be dangerous if it loses ground to a rival clan. Make sure you get along with everybody, even if your mentor is a mainstay of a clan or an active belligerent in an interdepartmental war.

Don't forget that, by the simple fact of being older, your mentor will probably leave the company before you do. Consequently you will end up alone, left to your own devices and potentially at the mercy of the enemies of your erstwhile mentor. Whatever you forced them to endure when you benefited from the protection of your mentor is likely to come back at you with interest. Once again, even if your mentor had some strained relationships within the company, you will be relatively spared from any reprisals if you have been kind and thoughtful with everyone. The departure of your mentor can make you dangerously vulnerable. Their successor might shunt you into a siding or even oust you from the company, thus dealing your career a fatal blow. Perhaps they want to promote their own protégé...

Most people who have been blessed with an experienced and trusted adviser will almost certainly attest to the strong connection that develops between mentor and mentee. As mentioned earlier in this book, connections such as these can take on a filial aspect. Once again you need to remember that your mentor is neither a guru nor your parent. Your mentor is not eternal. One day they will retire, move on to another company, or even get the sack... And you will be bereft of their benevolent aegis, pertinent advice and precious help. Their departure could isolate you if you counted solely on them. I have seen high-flying protégés suddenly drop like a stone when their mentors leave the company.

Some fall into a paralysing nostalgia, having forgotten that the time spent with their mentor was just another page in their life history. As with everything, the memory of your mentor will eventually be forgotten. You must put everything into perspective and keep a cool head.

It will be all the more necessary when, with your mentor gone from the company, you experience some serious turbulence. You will no longer benefit from their support and protection. You will probably have to go out and look for the opportunities that were once delivered to you on a plate. If your mentor helped you skip some rungs in your ascension of the company ladder, be warned that what you skipped might later turn out to be your Achilles heel. A good general should have ample experience of the battlefield, not just the comfort of army headquarters.

Having a mentor, a real one, is an incredible asset so long as you are aware of the associated risks and pitfalls which we looked at earlier in this chapter. A real mentor can boost your technical and social skills. They can help you perform better, excel and venture out of your comfort zone by affording you a sense of security.

Do you have the opportunity to collaborate with a real mentor? Seize that incredible chance before it slips through your fingers. You won't regret it.

3
Be Yourself, Be Responsible and Be In Control

3.1
Don't be a victim of fate

Every day you can hear at least one person explain how their problems are the fault of someone else.

"I'm not paid enough." "My boss is exploiting me." "They don't recognize my real worth." "Somebody else always gets the promotion." These are just some of the complaints I often hear, and here are some more: "I'm the wrong colour." "I'm the wrong nationality." "I'm a woman (or a man)." "I'm too old (or too young)." "I'm from the wrong class." "I'm under-qualified (or over-qualified)." "It's because of the slump." "It's the government's fault (regardless of its political persuasion)." "It's bad luck." "Fate has got it in for me." STOP!

Well if that is you, at some point you just have to accept the truth and stop justifying your failures or mediocrity as somebody else's fault. You also need to stop finding excuses for your own inactivity by blaming it on others or on fate.

If you are underpaid, you need to ask yourself whether your colleagues or opposite numbers in other companies are paid better. If they are, then why? If other companies pay better, why are you moaning about it instead of applying for a better-paid job?

So your boss is exploiting you. Is he or she like that with everyone, with certain employees or just you? Others are achieving but not you. What are the achievers doing differently to you?

What are you bringing to your company and, indirectly, to your boss? Do you bring in more than you cost? How much money have you generated for your company? How much money have you saved for your company? What have you improved in your company? And how much do you cost your company?

Rule number one: a company is not a charity. Its goal is to make a profit. If you cost more money than you generate, you are not contributing to the company's goal. So it wouldn't be surprising if you weren't getting a raise, because if you did, you would cost even more and would contribute even less to your company's goal. If that is your situation, don't even bother thinking about a promotion.

Never put your failures down to being the wrong sex, colour, class or nationality. Misogyny, racism and xenophobia are sadly all real and all part of human nature. I've come across them all, sometimes suffered, felt the anger and the pain. Such prejudices are the result of the instinctive fear of those who entertain them. It is the fear of having to face stiffer competition and, in short, lose what is considered to be a precious benefit. This asset could be a source of income (a job), a source of power, influence and control, a source of status... Those who discriminate against women are really just trying to put a lid on the potential competition. Those who discriminate against men are really just trying to fill the shoes of those who discriminate against women. Whites who discriminate against blacks – so they don't have to compete with them – are just the same as blacks discriminating against whites.

That's the real world. These prejudices are kept alive by people who place their primal survival instincts above their reason. They are also kept alive by others, especially cynical people, who want to use them and their attendant fears to achieve their own personal and very specific goals.

Such prejudices and fears can make the pursuit of your career more complicated but they shouldn't hold you back. You must overcome these difficulties and remain professional. Many women occupy positions of responsibility and great prestige. In my own career I have observed the same proportion of incompetence among men as among women. I've encountered incompetent blacks – and whites who are even more out of their depth. When you look at company bosses, you can't help but notice that they are rarely young. Margaret Thatcher was a woman but that didn't stop her becoming the Prime Minister of the United Kingdom. Neither did it stop Angela Merkel becoming the German chancellor or Édith Cresson leading the French government. Barack Obama is black and that didn't stop him becoming the president of the United States of America. So what is preventing you from enjoying a successful career? Just because the obstacles are more numerous does not mean that the task is impossible. It will just be more complicated. Sometimes it will be hard, disheartening, even alarming, but it will never be impossible, especially if others in a similar situation have already achieved success. Draw inspiration from them. In the end it is you who decides whether or not you rise to the challenge.

Focus on you, on your skills, and on your results. It doesn't matter if someone doesn't like your face. You will end up finding somebody who does. Prejudice is a blessing in disguise. Imagine you were recruited by someone who hates your colour or the fact that you are a woman, somebody who smiles broadly to your face but behind your back does their utmost to hinder your career, harm your prospects, humiliate you... Being unwelcome in a hell on earth is not a bad thing.

Each to his own career path and its associated obstacles. The only person running in this race is you. If you stumble and fall, it is because you didn't jump at the right time or correctly negotiate the obstacle. It wasn't the obstacle's fault. Analyse the reasons for your fall and think about how you are going to make the next jump. Get back up and start again. Keep starting again until you make it. It might hurt in the beginning – it probably will – but your perseverance will pay in the end.

Don't blame the circumstances into which you were born. While it is true that many rich people come from rich families, there are just as many who made their fortune after living modestly, even in poverty for many years. Warren Buffet lived for many long years with investments amounting to just a few thousand dollars. How many talented actors slogged away for years at minor roles before finally getting their name above the title?

Draw inspiration from their success. Learn from their story, the ordeals they had to overcome. Don't blame those who achieved success and don't hold them responsible for your personal failures, instead take inspiration from them. What did they do well? What did they do badly? What did they do that you haven't done or haven't thought of doing in your quest for success?

Your mind, your skills and above all your results will be the foundations of your success. Obstacles will always lie in your path and it is true that some encounter more than their fair share. No matter, they are part of the game, your game, and you must be its sole master. Nobody else but you should control your game. You will win thanks to you and only you. You will lose thanks to you, too. You should take responsibility for your actions and start again with the aim of doing better. And you should accept the consequences of your inactivity or your mistakes to better rectify them. Everybody knows that life is a game whose rules are particularly harsh. If some make it and you don't, it is because you lack some of the ingredients for success or you haven't gone about things correctly. Once again, draw inspiration from those who have achieved success. It might be that you are doing everything right but you are in the wrong place or it is the wrong time, perhaps even both. It might be that you are constantly repeating the same error without even realizing it. It has often happened to me and will certainly happen again. In my particular case, it usually takes the form of beliefs which aren't founded on any reality or rationality and which push me to undertake flawed actions, what some people call "cognitive biases", or other factors which I had hitherto ignored. My solution? Read and learn from others, as much as I can.

Achieving success implies that you come fully to terms with your situation and who you are. Hoping that tomorrow will be better will get you nowhere. Doing what you need to do to improve your lot will certainly lead you to better tomorrows. Waiting for the stars to align before taking action won't get you very far either, especially if you are waiting for a special astral event that only occurs every couple of centuries. Waiting for the government to find you a job or the funds to tide you over until that job falls into your lap is probably not the best way of going about achieving success.

Pull yourself together and take action. Only count on yourself. Nobody is responsible for your failure but you; nobody is responsible for your success but you. Draw inspiration from those who achieve success (not those who pretend to have achieved success), leave the miserable complaining to others, and don't fall for the destructive games of the frustrated and the toxic of every stripe.

Only those who take control of their lives, of their fate can achieve success. Those who defer to fate, to life's fortunes and the goodwill of others have practically no chance of achieving success and condemn themselves – through their inactivity – to being victims of their own destiny.

3.2
Be stronger than fear

No one really knows where fear comes from and how to control it. While fear might drive us to reacting well in certain situations, in others it can turn out to be particularly dangerous.

When we are faced with a predator, fear tends to paralyse us and fixes us to the spot. If the predator can only detect its prey when it moves, then all is well. If this isn't the case, you are going to be its next tasty snack.

Unfortunately for us most predators of the human race, and this includes viruses, do not locate us through our movements. And unfortunately for most of us who live in the modern world, we run a greater risk of falling victim to our fellow creatures than to any other type of predator.

The greatest danger for a company is to do nothing. Time affects us like weather erosion on a stone or inflation on your savings. Survival and success are not about waiting around to see what will happen, but about taking action.

However fear will hold us back, even prevent us from taking action. Only your reason can convince you it is time to take action. And the reasoning is simple.

The first option is to do nothing. For the moment all's well, you are safe within your comfort zone and satisfied with your routine. Your salary gets paid every month and perhaps there is a bonus at the end of the year. You let time do the heavy lifting, avoid taking risks, and don't really attempt to make any progress. Each month your salary covers your expenses. Your lack of risk-taking eliminates all anxiety. You drowse and languish contentedly in this cosy and reassuring environment, like a passenger on a cruise liner. You might be lucky and continue placidly in this state until the end of your days, enjoying your company's generosity until your retirement, then a generous state pension topped up by a healthy pension fund.

However in all likelihood things won't pan out that way. Unemployment can befall you at any moment and, if you are not financially independent, your tranquil cruise will turn into a titanic nightmare. The older you are, the more difficult it will be to bounce back. Don't forget those cheaper young rivals snapping at your heels. They are hungry and gaining on you in terms of competencies and experience. Don't forget, too, the international competition which is thirsty for knowledge and which, year on year, consolidates its skills and quality. Don't forget your superiors are under pressure from the shareholders and need to reduce costs, such as yourself, to maintain their own position. They might even get a bonus based on the savings made from firing you. Don't overlook the latest fads, new techniques and technology, short and long-lived economic crises, and accidental injuries. If you are 50 years old, unemployed and not financially independent, you risk ending up like the legions of unemployed executives masquerading as consultants who play a role as pathetic as it is tragic. And how do you finance a lifespan longer than your forebears with a social security system reduced to a mere shadow of its former self? When that realization hits home, you will kick yourself for having done nothing about it. Even colossal efforts to rectify the situation might not be enough to make up for the lost time and soothe your regrets. The fear of taking immediate action will be replaced by a chronic fear of the future which will, with every passing year, increase its hold over you.

The other option, a much nicer one, is the one advocated by this book: get yourself out of your comfort zone and take calculated risks to further your career. At the start you will undoubtedly be subject to little rushes of adrenaline and stress generated by the changes. But your successes, although modest in the beginning, will soon give you a taste for the thrill. You will gain in self-confidence and come to the conclusion that it wasn't as difficult as all that. Little by little you will get better at it, borne along by a virtuous circle. You will feel proud of yourself. Probably your loved ones will too, inspired by your example. You will become resistant to stress, stronger within and calmer as your new-found mental fortitude enables you to take control of your life. A certain number of your ambitions and dreams can thus be realized, reducing proportionally your future regrets.

Taking action is what makes you forget about your fear.

Inactivity will sustain and increase your fear.

Commit yourself to reading twenty pages a day, as in twenty sides of ten sheets of paper, and over the course of a year you will read twenty-four 300-page books. That's huge. Twenty-four well-chosen books can boost your skills and mindset, and put you firmly on the road to success. If you do that over five years, that is 120 books. Books will help you clarify the uncertainty that frightens you. They will put new cards into your hand and make you a better player, one who is prepared for the game and more self-confident. Books will provide reassurance by showing you that some people started out with much less and nevertheless achieved enormous success after having overcome numerous obstacles, some of which might even not bear thinking about. So if they made it to the top, why not you? You aren't less intelligent.

Distance yourself from people who perpetuate your fear and who get a depraved kick out of it.

These two simple actions will help you bump-start a virtuous circle that will enable you to achieve success. These two simple actions will also help you dispel the fear that paralyses you naturally and easily.

Something or someone that impresses, can cause fear. So don't allow yourself to be easily impressed. All that glistens isn't necessarily gold. Grey hairs aren't necessarily a sign of experience. Fancy clothes and a luxury car aren't proof of material wealth. A large prestigious company might employ mediocre staff or be losing money, while a more modestly sized business might have brilliant employees and a generate profits of 30% year in year out. Find out as much as you can by digging deep and comparing several sources of information, and you will surely gain a truer picture. It is the same for personal success. Follow the advice of people like Ray Dalio and Warren Buffet rather than listen to a YouTuber in a bedsit explaining how to make a fortune.

Concerning the subject of fear, I would like to draw your attention to one final aspect. It is a strange feeling, unpleasant, and one that generates fear for no apparent reason. I lived with this feeling for quite some time and it also dawned on me that many of the brilliant people I know have also experienced it, again for no apparent reason. Specialists have given this strange feeling a name: impostor syndrome. I find it hard to describe this condition which, regardless of your skills and legitimacy, makes you feel like a fraud, like you don't have the right to be where you are or aren't up to the job you are supposed to be doing. Time and effort will be your best allies in defeating this syndrome. Put in the work so you know everything about your remit, all the ins and outs of it, and then call on experts to help you develop solutions to the various problems it throws in your path. Slowly but surely you will reduce the intensity of your imposter syndrome. Your successes, which can but only accumulate in proportion to the effort you put in, will chip away at the last remaining traces of this unpleasant condition until one fine day you will find, like I did, that it is all just a bad memory.

3.3
Know how to roll with the blows

Your chances of achieving success will be greater if you are standing on your own two feet rather than lying flat on your back.

Just as in their private lives, many people resign themselves to their fate and give up too quickly when faced with difficulties in their professional endeavours. But hard knocks are a part of life. Some just hurt, some can hurt a lot, and some will stop you dead in your tracks and get you thinking the darkest of thoughts.

If you are to survive and succeed, you need absolutely to develop perseverance and endurance. If at every setback – if indeed it really is a setback – you give up then you have practically no chance of either surviving or succeeding.

Do you want to survive in the workplace? Do you want to succeed? Well, be prepared to take the knocks, slip on the banana skins and suffer the stabs in the back, especially if you want not only to survive but to achieve tangible, meaningful success. The competition is fierce and your affable colleagues are not necessarily as nice as they lead you to believe. You are going to have to prepare yourself like a professional boxer.

Many of us react instead of thinking ahead, which is a serious mistake. The person who reacts is not in control of the game but at its mercy. When you play, you should anticipate your opponent's likely reactions and attacks. Depending on your opponent's possibilities, what situation are you going to find yourself in? How are you going to cope? How are you going to benefit? How are you going to win? The answer is you need to get to know your opponents and that takes time. In the meantime it is normal and perfectly natural for them to score a few points and you, none. The element of surprise will initially work against you but, with time, you will get a handle on how they operate, what and how they attack, their techniques, their tricks… This will allow you to prepare and then you can draw them on to ground which is more favourable to you.

I recall a manager in another department who took part in all the strategic meetings. He systematically – and sometimes aggressively – challenged those present on the basis of abstract principles and never on concrete details. He was an avid reader of management journals published by the leading universities and business schools, written by theoreticians who have never run a company or made the slightest strategic decision but who nevertheless explain how to manage your organization using a spreadsheet or a pyramid diagram. Despite living in his theoretical world, this manager had the executive committee's ear which afforded him a certain power to cause trouble. Many people simply did their best to avoid him so they didn't have to suffer his criticisms and humiliations in public.

Right from the start he clearly despised me and ranked me as one the idiots because I wasn't interested in his pyramids and spreadsheets devoid of meaningful figures. On several occasions he criticized my own projects for various reasons: "No alternative project" or "No strengths and weaknesses analysis." His remarks were regular and predictable. Nevertheless I managed to get every one of my projects approved because they were simple and if they failed, the company had nothing to lose. In the end all the projects that I managed to move forward despite his barrage of criticisms turned out to be profitable, and I didn't hesitate to point it out to him. In subsequent meetings I began by looking him straight in the eye and announcing that I didn't have an alternative project to offer, no strengths and weaknesses analysis to present, but a new opportunity similar to the previous ones which all produced good results. He never challenged me again after that. Two years later his employment was terminated for a lack of results.

People like him are easy to manage. Others are more twisted.

Some will appropriate your work. Like the manager who discreetly purloined the deal I had successfully negotiated and then presented it to her superiors as an exceptional opportunity for the company. Her boss told me about this new better and cheaper service she had managed to pull off. I couldn't believe my ears. I invited her boss into my office and pulled out all my files from the negotiation to show him that it was in fact me who had sealed the extraordinary deal three years before. I mentioned this incident in passing during discussions with various managers and members of the executive committee. Her reputation was sealed.

Others will make mistakes and then palm them off on you. I remember a certain manager of another department who caused me a lot of trouble on a particular project. His arguments didn't hold up to scrutiny and on several occasions he explained to me that the decision for putting the project on hold wasn't his but one of the executive directors', who was my superior. The situation it created exposed the company and me to a certain number of risks. So I went to see this executive director, my boss, and explained the situation. He immediately hit the roof, sternly demanding who could have approved such a stupid decision. When I showed him the manager's emails accusing him, the executive director, of being the decision maker, he was furious. The next day, everything was resolved and the company rid itself permanently of the manager's incompetence.

Others will pretend that your work has been done poorly, such as the employee in my team who, without my knowledge, seized every opportunity to harm my reputation. One day he went to see my boss with the express purpose of showing him that my calculations didn't add up, that my lack of rigour was putting the company in danger. It was true, I had a difference of $6,000 on a total sum of two billion dollars, but these were estimates which by their very nature could never be absolutely accurate. It afforded me the opportunity to mention that this person understood nothing of the work he was trying to rubbish, and that my error amounted to 0.0003% of the total budget, which was an excellent result for an estimate.

There is also the manager who serves no real purpose but presents your work to his superiors like a true expert. You do the hard graft, he or she gets the praise (and never shares it with you). Managers of this type are even more dangerous if you let them play their game because when the day comes to lay a few people off, they won't hesitate to say that you are useless and that he or she is the only expert. I knew one like that. Every time I did a job and he was going to present it as his own, I made sure that his boss and many other people in the company were aware of what I was working on and the good results it produced. So when he was thinking he was presenting a scoop, his boss was in fact already aware of the precise details. Even worse for him, I made sure to inform his boss of the weaknesses and opportunities inherent in each project so when the time came, the boss could pick him up on the negatives and suggest avenues to explore for even greater success. Most amusing of all, my manager often returned from these ordeals in an execrable mood from the humiliation he had just received, and was totally oblivious to the fact that I had been in prior contact with his boss and perhaps other people in the meeting. He would tell me to do what his boss had suggested. He would ask me the questions I had gone through with his boss. One day this manager came up with a restructuring plan which involved laying me off. Aware that it was in fact I who was doing the heavy lifting, the executive fired him and kept me on. And the manager was once again at a total loss as to the reason for his superior's decision, considering it to be a wholly unfair dismissal.

And I could mention numerous other occasions where I received a blow below the belt. Each time I had to roll with the punches, and the humiliation. But it doesn't mean you have to learn to enjoy the knocks. Instead, learn lessons from your mistakes and above all, learn not to repeat them. The examples you have just read show how I learned to dodge the bullets and turn the tables on my adversaries, using their own dishonesty, greed, pride, contempt, incompetence and foolishness against them to great effect.

And I did it without imitating their ways of operating, without getting involved in their depraved games, and without betraying my own principles. Each of the above-mentioned situations was a success, a victory over pettiness and base human nature, and of that I am proud. These successes have cleansed me of the hurt and humiliation caused by the mean minded. They have made me stronger and have contributed positively to my reputation.

3.4
Be opportunistic and daring

As the saying goes, "all things come to those who wait". The problem is you can wait and wait, but often nothing comes.

Those who do nothing are in fact waiting. They are hoping, dreaming, procrastinating. They are waiting for luck. Fortunes might come to those who chose the right numbers in the national lottery. That promotion at work wasn't for me this time, they chose somebody else, but we'll see what happens next year. Their relationship isn't going very well but they will wait and see, perhaps it will be better next year. They are unhappy, but some are in an even worse situation. They can't find work because the current economic situation is difficult but like the government says, it might be better next year. More often than not they turn out to be very creative when it comes to inventing excuses for not doing anything or justifying their inactivity.

And then there are those who take action. They have dreams too, but instead of hoping that their luck will change, they take action and do their utmost to make them real. For them, fortunes are made by figuring out how to increase their income and grow their savings by investing them wisely. They educate and train themselves continuously. If they are unhappy in their relationship, they take action by discussing their problems with their spouse and then look for suitable solutions, which could be to divorce but at least they do something. They don't allow the situation to deteriorate until it is painful for everybody involved. If the job market is moribund, they look for ways to stand out and connect directly with the people who are hiring. If they are unhappy and don't want to be, they look to happy people for insight and inspiration, and then take action. They don't place their confidence in the lottery or the government to make them a fortune or find a job. They don't look for excuses for not taking action or justifying their idleness. Their fate isn't the neighbour's fault but resides instead in their own hands. They know this and take control of their life accordingly.

Those who achieve success are generally opportunists in that they know how to seize an opportunity when it presents itself. If they miss one, they will try to make up for it the following time. If opportunities are scarce, they focus their energy on the rare ones that exist, trying to replicate them or even create new ones.

Some look for opportunities at all costs, even to the detriment of others or the group, which means their happiness is founded on someone else's loss. Such opportunists are destructive and toxic. They are the ones who try to trip you up, appropriate your work by putting their name on it, spread rumours about you, massage facts and figures to achieve success... And there are a lot of them. Some despise themselves for it, others are proud of their cynical efforts which they consider to be the mark of a superior intelligence and admire themselves in the bathroom mirror every morning before setting off to accomplish their dirty work. Personally I have never understood how such people manage to be at peace with themselves, and I avoid their sort like the plague.

Others are also opportunists but, as I have already explained, they would never pursue success to the detriment of their neighbour. Instead they would try to achieve success without collateral damage, in an honest fashion. And if their opportunity benefits others or – better still – the wider population, they will feel happy about themselves and work even harder to rise to the challenge ahead of them. If you manage to pull off an operation that gives you a decent return, but also gives a decent return to your superiors, your colleagues and your company, then you should be proud of yourself.

Being daring will help you generate opportunities and bring them to fruition. It is a useful trait of character but one that requires the courage necessary to leave your comfort zone and take calculated risks. It certainly doesn't mean being impetuous. Daring means knowing how to go that step further to achieve something that might increase your security or enable you to seize an opportunity.

Be bold, be daring! Dare to propose new ideas. Dare to speak to your manager or your manager's manager. Dare to admit your mistakes and undertake to rectify them. Dare to defend your point of view and learn to back it up with solid arguments. Dare to say "No" when you don't want to say "Yes". Do you rarely do anything daring because of fear? This is normal. Start by suggesting to your manager a simple project to improve the organization of your department. Explain to them the problem, how much it costs the company in time and money, what you propose to do about it and a provisional schedule for the various stages of the project. Put your heart into the project and drive it forward using your intelligence and energy until you succeed. The next time, aim a little higher. The time after that, make it an even bigger goal. And when you position becomes too limited for major undertakings, make an appointment with your manager's manager or the director of human resources and offer your services to another department. Make sure you have all the necessary evidence to highlight your achievements. What if there aren't any opportunities in your company? Look elsewhere. Whatever the case, you will have certainly gained the courage and daring you need to advance your career.

3.5
Be mobile

We have already seen in this book how being static, immobile in an organization makes you vulnerable. You considerably increase your risk of being impacted by a redundancy scheme or mass lay-off. Taking action is therefore a key factor in increasing your chances of survival and success.

Mobility is also geographical. Many choose not to move for numerous reasons, because it is easier, more comfortable, because of family pressure, or just because they love their home region. And yet accepting assignments or a job in another region or perhaps another country is an effective way of boosting your career.

When I finished my higher education, I remember seeing most of the students get jobs within a thirty-kilometre radius of our university. They found interesting jobs paying above-average salaries, often in internationally renowned companies or institutions. A minority chose not to stay and headed for the provinces or went abroad.

Twenty years later the comparison was striking. Those who had stayed tended to stagnate. Certainly they had positions of responsibility and were well paid, but most of them remained close to their starting point in terms of duties, promotion and remuneration.

Those who had moved to the provinces didn't necessarily have better salaries than those who had remained, simply because salaries aren't generally as high outside the big cities. On the other hand most of them ended up having greater responsibilities and higher positions in the company hierarchy. And even if the bottom line of their payslip was similar, or perhaps even lower, their purchasing power was still greater and their job more interesting.

As for those who had gone abroad, as I had done, because an opportunity had presented itself or they hadn't found a job that suited them at home, they enjoyed a dazzling career progression both in terms of rank and remuneration. Many made it into the executive committee or found themselves working closely with the directors of a major group, whereas those who had stayed near the university found themselves coming up against a glass ceiling within their departments. The difference in pay was easily doubled or tripled at the very least. And here is the curious thing: when they came home, those who had had international experience were offered positions that were inaccessible to those who had stayed!

Yet we all had the same qualifications.

For those who have gained experience and aren't afraid of moving far away from home, working in another country is an interesting solution. Not only do you generally get paid a higher salary than in your native country, your company might even pay your taxes, take care of your accommodation, fund you children's education, cover your health insurance premiums, and reimburse a certain number of your expenses. In fact, you could find yourself in a situation where your entire salary is tantamount to just one big personal savings scheme. And the cherry on the cake, your home country probably wouldn't tax your income at all. Of course, as an expatriate you could find yourself comfortably installed in a major city which offers a very pleasant living and working environment. However, working abroad often involves less appealing destinations, sometimes in countries which attract few foreigners. Hence the excellent financial conditions to encourage potential applicants to take the plunge. Working overseas is also a good way of furthering your career. Take for example the head chef I encountered in the kitchen of a prestigious Beijing hotel. Despite having worked in a well-known luxury hotel and having acquired his experience in celebrated establishments across the globe, in his home country his career would have plateaued at second chef.

Moving overseas to countries calling out for specialists with your skills set is always going to be an excellent opportunity. Not only will you be able to fulfil your potential, occupying positions you would never have imagined possible at home, you will also enjoy the trappings of a generous salary and comfortable living conditions. The experience might be hard at first because of the new environment, the language, the culture, the different ways of working... but you will soon adapt yourself to the situation. You might even find that you never want to go home, which is something that happens to many expats regardless of their country of origin.

If you have acquired experience in your field, feel that promotion is out of reach, or are just bored in your present company, you should seriously consider the possibility of working overseas. Are you single? If the answer is "Yes", then it couldn't be simpler. If you are married and your spouse has a good job or strong family ties, the situation becomes more complicated. If your spouse lacks prospects in your potential destination, they risk becoming depressed while you are fulfilling your dreams.

I chose to move overseas and I have never regretted that decision. It boosted my career, my salary, gave me financial independence, enabled me to build a life that I wouldn't have been able to do in my home country for want of opportunities and above all, it allowed me to live several lives in one. Your career is more than just a professional experience, it is an adventure, a life adventure.

It doesn't matter if you are an engineer, a financier, a qualified technician, a lawyer or a craftsman, the adventure of working overseas is always an option. What counts is that your expertise is lacking somewhere else in the world and that you are ready to live an exceptional adventure.

3.6
Be respectful

It feels pleasant when you are acknowledged and respected, doesn't it? We all need to feel that others recognize our existence, in any case that is what I believe.

And yet every day I see people who can't be bothered to say "Please", to reward the person holding the door open with a "Thank you" or to simply reply to somebody's "Hello". When someone shuts the door in my face, fails to say please or ignores my greeting, it affects me and might even engender a certain feeling of hostility towards the person responsible.

Acknowledging a greeting with a greeting – and a smile – contributes to creating a positive atmosphere around you. Adding a "How are you today?" or a "How's your family?" and you will contribute to establishing a benevolent atmosphere around you.

That way, the empathy you generate will reduce the number of hostile or potentially hostile individuals around you, as well as capitalizing on your image. With a bit of luck, you could even become an example for others who might not necessarily be unpleasant but just a bit shy. With a few well-placed words and a smile, you could break the ice for everyone around you.

A final point: if empathy isn't your thing and you are an out-and-out cynic, you mustn't forget that the little person you despised today might be the only person who reaches out to you when you need help tomorrow.

3.7
Be precise, concise and reliable: be professional

One of my biggest problems in the past was that my presentations were all about what interested me and not about what interested the person I was presenting to. I was motivated by a desire to demonstrate the high quality of my work and the extent of my skills, in the greatest detail and not without some little pride. It was pretty dire. The truth of it was the members of my audience had to sit through a tsunami of information that didn't interest them. Worse, I was wasting their time, failing to address their concerns and ending up completely discrediting myself by acting like scatterbrained professor.

You should develop a supplier-customer approach to your communication, even when talking to your company colleagues. You are the supplier. The company's customers are customers. The people you work for in the company are also (in-house) customers, and you should give them what they expect from you and nothing else.

First of all, objectively identify who your customer is. Usually your in-house customer is your boss, perhaps even your boss's boss. Who is he or she? What does they want (bonus, promotion, glory)? What are the problems facing them right now? What are the results they need?

With those questions answered, you can then target your presentation using the following key steps.

1) Clearly describe the problem or issue that is facing the company and, indirectly, your boss and his hierarchy.
2) Explain in simple terms your solution and how it will benefit the company and, indirectly, implicitly, your boss and his hierarchy.
3) Detail the costs and the schedule for implementing your solution, including a margin for safety (always be conservative in your estimates).

4) List all the associated risks and solutions for avoiding them.

5) Include everything else in appendices or keep it handy for the questions at the end (sources, data, method, etc.).

Make sure your presentation is done and dusted in ten minutes. Any longer, and you will lose the attention of your audience and run the risk of people asking all sorts of questions which will make you lose the thread of your speech. Just a ten-minute presentation, simple, clear, and without going into the details. The rest of your allotted time will be for the questions, the details, the methods, the risks, and so on.

You don't present a solution, you sell it. You sell yourself. You are selling yourself continuously. Your survival in the company is a tacit renewal of your employment contract. That contract can be broken at any moment. If the contract continues to run, it is because the company (through your hierarchy) has the financial resources and the desire to keep you. Your contract is founded on a multitude of tacit contracts that you make with your hierarchy to ensure your survival in the company. Many employees think that they only have to sell themselves during their initial job interview. That is a dangerous illusion. You are selling yourself continuously. You are implicitly renewing (and improving) your employment contract continuously.

You have no more than three minutes to complete steps 1 and 2. Quite often the decision will be made before you even get to step 3.

When someone asks you a question, answer clearly. Wherever possible, answer "Yes" or "No" and explain rapidly why. Avoiding saying ambiguous phrases such as "Yes and no", "Maybe, maybe not" and "It depends". If doubts persist, make it clear that it is "Yes" or "No". Are you uncertain or unable to answer? Don't make it up, instead explain that you don't have all the elements you need to give an answer right now, and will have to tie up those loose ends before saying more. If your subsequent research fails to provide you with a yes or a no answer, draw up a list of the pros and cons in two separate columns. On this basis, you can make a guesstimate (and you should say clearly that is what it is) that in all likelihood the answer is "Yes".

You get asked for a report? Make sure you include a summary on the first page which simply and factually details steps 1 and 2. You, the writer, will probably be the only person who reads the entire report. Those who receive the report will read the summary and might take a look at some key paragraphs.

Writing a report requires adhering to some simple rules. The list of contents should state clearly what is in the report. The summary should present the main points of the report and convince the reader of the proposal's merits. The heading of each section should summarize its contents. Each paragraph should convey an idea. The first sentence of each paragraph summarizes the paragraph. By reading the first sentence of a paragraph, the reader should be able to develop an understanding of its contents. If the reader wants to learn more, he or she can read the following sentences in the paragraph. Use an appendix to indicate your sources, your method, your theories, and so on. The reader should be able to understand your report just by reading the list of contents or the summary. They should be convinced of its merits simply by reading the list of contents or the summary. But how do you know if it is convincing? Test it on yourself. Imagine for a moment that you are your boss, someone who has ambitions and has to deal with problems. Then read the list of contents. Are you convinced? Then read the summary. Are you convinced? If not, then your boss probably won't be convinced either. Go back to work.

Don't talk about concepts, instead provide precise figures, backed with evidence, and propose practical solutions and actions. Do you have an idea to minimize a fall in sales? Get the attention of your boss in the lift with a pitch like this: "Good morning. I've seen the sales figures. This 16% fall over three months is worrying. I've gone through the issue with some of our specialists and I think we can minimize the fall to 12%. Are you interested?" Before the lift doors open, you can be sure they will invite you to make an appointment with their secretary. From that moment on, the rest is up to you.

Each figure, each problem and each solution mentioned in steps 1 to 4 must be meticulously researched. Where do these figures come from? How were they calculated? What hypotheses have you inferred from them? What is your reasoning? What could cause your plan to fail? How? None of this should appear in your speech or your presentation of steps 1 to 4; instead, put it in the appendix or make it available to anyone wishing to go into further detail. Just like the buyer of a car is more interested in its design, comfort, quality and safety rather than how the combustion engine works, your purchaser, in other words your in-house customer will only be interested in the aspects they consider important. If they ask you to explain how it works, then and only then do you lift up the bonnet.

Work that is rock solid, has been well researched, has nothing to hide, and presents the tangible and quantifiable results clearly and simply, is the work of a professional.

Take the example of a pizza delivery service which has a problem: 27% of its customers complain that their orders aren't hot when they arrive. These customers amount to 22% of sales. You talk to the delivery team and they all say that the pizzas come straight out of the kitchen and into their delivery bags, piping hot. The kitchen staff confirm this. Unfortunately the delivery guys get delayed in the evening traffic. You have personally tested a new GPS system which optimizes travel times so effectively that you can expect to save an average of ten minutes on every trip. The cost of fitting out the delivery team with this new GPS, and thus securing the loyalty of those 22% of unsatisfied customers, is less than 1% of the company's turnover. If the situation doesn't improve, these customers would certainly look elsewhere for their favourite food. What's more, if you manage to secure the loyalty of those customers, they would probably recommend your pizzas to their friends and family... Investing 1% of turnover in order to retain 22% of the clientele and probably gain new customers in the process is a no-brainer: the figures speak for themselves. The solution is simple, clearly profitable, and quick and easy to implement. Let's do it! And don't forget to ask for a bonus or a promotion once the results confirm the plan has worked.

Many very competent technicians, sometimes graduating from the most prestigious schools, are poor communicators and don't know how to sell themselves. As a result they miss opportunities which often go to less qualified technicians who know how to sell themselves. Whether you are an engineer, a lawyer, a technician, an economist or a financier, you need to be technically good but you also need to know how to sell yourself. Study sales techniques. You will learn how to sell your ideas and projects by convincing your audience simply and effectively.

It will also help you if, one day, you have to sell yourself on the job market. You need to understand what your potential new employer expects (step 1), show him or her you are the solution using verifiable figures (step 2), discuss timing, the resources at your disposal and pay (step 3).

In short, you need to be technically competent regardless of your role and position in the hierarchy. You need to communicate concisely and effectively on the facts and the results your customers expect to obtain. And don't forget this: the best person to sell your services is you.

3.8
Be disciplined… and lazy

What are your qualities? One of mine is that I am lazy.

Lazy is exactly what I am. I always try to minimize the time I spend on a task or assignment. The time saved can then be devoted to other projects, including personal ones, as well as to my family, pastimes, education, rest and relaxation.

In my work I try to be lazy for other people too. If during the course of my assignment I come across an opportunity for saving other people's time, I seize it. And of course I make sure everybody knows.

A recent example concerned the renewal of the insurance policies covering the commercial group where I work. This task required at least several days, perhaps even several weeks' work for each one of our subsidiaries, and of course the latter also had plenty of other projects to deal with. Considering the number of subsidiaries and the average cost per hour of an employee, this particularly boring but very necessary task cost the company heaps of money. By simplifying the organization, by using a standard format for gathering the data, by collecting much of the information from existing reports, we managed to reduce the workload to an average of a half-day per year for each subsidiary. This saved the subsidiaries a considerable amount of time, and made a lot of people happy because they no longer had to sacrifice their working hours to this pretty unrewarding task every year. As for the savings made, the executive committee were particularly appreciative because these were recurrent costs, coming round every year.

I know many brilliant people who have a very disciplined approach to life. I noticed that this self-control made them very efficient and productive people. A balanced and healthy diet, getting up early, working out before heading to the office, optimizing their schedule, setting time aside for reading, going to bed early and at a regular time... Discipline such as this helps keep them at the top of their game.

Unfortunately for me I have never managed to adhere to such a strict lifestyle for very long, and while I perform well, I know that my lack of discipline holds me back from reaching the very top. While I focus on the quality of my sleep, eat a pretty balanced diet, read a lot and so on, I share Winston Churchill's views on sport and tend to linger under the covers in the morning, especially in the winter. My diary isn't managed with military precision either. But that is a personal choice and even if I could achieve more through more personal discipline, I like my lifestyle the way it is. Each to his own when it comes to finding the balance between performance and lifestyle.

Nevertheless, when it comes to ethics and results (properly costed, of course), I am very disciplined. On these points, laziness is wholly inappropriate. For a start, your reputation is at stake. It takes many years to build one, but just a few hours to demolish it entirely. Also, while some achieve great financial riches without troubling themselves with the ethics of their success, it is far better to be able to look at oneself in the mirror every morning and see someone who is at peace with the world and free of regrets.

Laziness helps me be efficient, not waste time and instead save it. Laziness helps me be creative, find solutions for doing more, faster. These solutions contribute to making profits for the company and consequently to my own success. My laziness has helped me filter tasks and forced me to focus only on what is necessary and what can help me achieve success. My laziness has helped me filter the people around me, whom I spend time with, discarding the useless and the toxic in favour of people who really count and who add something to my life.

As crazy as it might sound, laziness is a force which motivates me and helps me achieve success. It reminds me of the economics lectures at university which defined efficiency as "Obtaining as much as possible through as little effort as possible". I call it "positive laziness" in opposition to the negative sort which prevents you from taking action, which encourages you to remain inactive in a comfortable bubble and hope it won't all blow up in your face...

3.9
Know how to give in order to receive

A true professional does business. He or she knows how to invest, that is to say, how to give in order to receive more. True professionals know that nothing is free. They know that they will never make it on their own, but need other people's help and skills.

A company isn't at all like a large family, despite what some might say. In general if you give nothing then you get nothing in return, except for being labelled as stingy, petty, tight-fisted, penny-pinching... As a rule these types never radiate happiness and their narrow-mindedness often condemns them, in the best of cases, to minor managerial roles.

If you want to succeed you need to know how to invest, particularly in people.

Want to protect a patent properly? Employ a lawyer who specializes in protecting patents. Want to develop your business in another country? Recruit a team locally and use a local accountancy firm. Want to review your tax strategy? Call on recognized specialists in the field. Sometimes it can be expensive. However deciding to dispense with expert advice could cost you much more in the long run and might even put you in a perilous situation. My grandmother's favourite maxim was "Cheap always ends up costing more than expensive". When I was 7 years old, I didn't really understand what she meant. Nowadays it is perfectly clear in my mind.

Also invest some of your time in improving your relations with people whom you have to collaborate closely with, or who might be able to help you in some capacity. A lunch or a beer after work are simple gestures that can bear abundant fruit. Moments such as these allow both of you to appreciate the other, to talk about subjects both professional and personal. You will gain a better insight into your colleagues' ideas, opinions, skills and personality. Some people will disappoint you. Some will remain neutral towards you. Others will become close collaborators who will help you (often unreservedly) in the projects you undertake. Any group of close associates that you can bring together in this way will be a precious resource in your pursuit of success.

Avoid management consultants unless of course you have no other option. Their interest in prolonging as much as possible their assignment and charging you top whack risks blowing a hole in your budget and your reputation. In addition to their great cost, they will also contribute to maintaining you in your comfort zone, to keeping you static. And we know that comfort is only comfortable in the short and medium terms, and becomes decidedly dangerous in the long run. You should continuously educate yourself and acquire new skills if you want to keep ahead. And yet it is often the consultant who gets to learn and not you. The consultant eats up your budget, learns, gets more competent with every assignment – and you? You start costing more and more for your company, learn little and stagnate in terms of acquiring new skills.

If you use the services of a consultant, use him or her to coach you and acquire new skills. How do they go about their job? What are their sources, their methods, their tips...? Learn from him or her and then apply what you have learnt to your own business. You will no longer need the consultant for simple assignments because you will be able to manage on your own. From thereon use the consultant for more complex assignments and continue the process. It'll be one of those proverbial win-win situations because you will increase your skills base and the company will make substantial savings. Nothing but good news for your survival and progress.

3.10
Be a business facilitator

In meetings, I've lost count of the number of times I've heard phrases such as "It isn't possible", "We've never done that before", "We don't have the resources" and "It's risky". And how many times have phrases like these led to missed opportunities? Countless times.

One of the fundamental rules in a company is this: don't block or hinder business. You should facilitate business as much as possible, in the same way that you should take care to ensure the safety and ethics of your dealings.

When the manager of another department comes to see you for a project or a problem you can help them with, never turn them away. Listen to them first. If the subject is completely out of your control and you can do nothing for them, explain clearly the reasons why and point them in the direction of the right person. If the subject concerns you, look into it. Don't hesitate to ask for time to study the question, listen to other points of view, and gather the necessary data so that you can form your own opinion.

Is the subject of the meeting a problem? Don't associate yourself with the problem, only the solution. Analyse the problem, look for the simplest solution for everybody, secure a consensus for setting it up and then implement it. In the case of a very complex problem, make sure you are – very visibly – part of the working group tasked with solving it.

Is the subject an opportunity for developing the business or improving it? It might feel like an opportunity worth seizing, but be prudent. Analyse the situation. Who is asking for your help? What is their reputation like? What have they achieved previously? What kind of person are they? Next, does the idea come from that person or from someone higher up? From whom? And what is at stake? What are the benefits in terms of money and status? What efforts are required? The risk is you do all the work and the person who came to you for help claims all the rewards. If the opportunity seems to be a good one, work with this person but stay visible and make sure you are recognized for your true value in meetings, reports and presentations. You will score points, but you will also garner recognition and new allies. You will strengthen your group of close collaborators in the company, as well as your position and your reputation. In short, you will strengthen everything you need to survive and succeed in the company.

Let's return to the subject of meetings where opportunities can be shot down by dismissive remarks. If senior executives are at the meeting, it is a chance for you to score points and stand out from the crowd. When somebody launches a missile across the table to shoot down an opportunity, everybody in the room usually falls silent and then passes on to the next subject. If you think the opportunity is worthwhile, realistic and viable, this is the moment for you to make a play. Once the dismissive remark has been uttered, in the brief moment of silence that follows, you can refute it or at least minimize its effects. First, ask for a couple of key figures, for example the sums which could be earned or saved, from the minimum to the maximum. Are competitors studying or developing this particular opportunity? If the game seems to be worth the candle, offer to look into it, to study the question in greater detail, with of course the approval of the decision makers in the room. If it turns out to be a non-starter, you will have just wasted a bit of your time. If on the other hand there is something to be done, and it is often the case, you can score a considerable number of points for your career. And don't forget, your enterprising spirit will certainly not be lost on the decision makers who, one day when they need somebody, might well think of you...

As a general rule, never block an initiative without first taking the time to understand it. If you feel it may involve risks or sticking points, make the observation that the subject is a complex one and you will look into it. It is up to you to find the solutions. If none of the possible solutions seems viable, explain why in detail but also show them you have done your utmost to make it work. Nobody will blame you for it.

People who block business risk paying a high price. The company must move forward to survive and develop, which is what its senior executives endeavour to do. And that is why they need reliable people at their side. If you are a hindrance, they will try to get rid of you. Additionally, if you create more problems than you solve, you will develop a bad reputation which risks sealing your fate the next time the company is restructured. Last of all, all those people you have blocked, hindered or frustrated will never forget you, and when the fateful day arrives, probably without you realizing it, the consensus will be for elbowing you aside or even pushing you out of the door.

3.11
Inspire people

Enjoying success within a company often requires taking on – to a greater or lesser degree depending on the position you occupy in the company – the role of leader.

We won't turn this book into a leadership manual, but it is worthwhile going through some of the key factors which have helped me successfully play this role in situations where previously nobody would have followed me.

The first thing to consider is trust. If you are known for your credibility and honesty, you will inspire confidence in people and they will trust you. If you are someone people listen to, if your expertise is recognized, if your initiatives are generally met with success, then you will inspire confidence both in terms of your technical abilities and your professionalism.

The second point involves the rewards that others hope to enjoy. Why should others bother following you and make a great effort if the results are meagre? Every effort should be rewarded and you should personally make sure that it happens. This isn't simply a question of greed but, once again, a rule of business: you must give to receive. You need to ask yourself about the project's usefulness, what is it going to achieve? How much is it going to cost the company? What problems will it solve? The chosen undertaking needs to be meaningful, and you will need to convince the participating players that their efforts have a purpose. Also, recognition and glory are rewards that all of us appreciate receiving. And of course money and promotion are coveted recompenses which help the recipients progress and keep the wolf from the door.

When I commit to a project I usually require the help of people who are skilled in a variety of fields. Either I already know who they are and go to see them directly, or I go through their manager or head of department. If I am to take it on, the project always has to motivate me, generate value and, ideally, be aligned with one or several of the executive committee's concerns.

I don't have the power to promote or raise the salaries of those who help me, even if the project is a successful one. But what I can do is offer my helpers time, my time. And I use my time in various ways. For example, I can go to see a senior executive to congratulate him or her on the work done by a department under their supervision, and highlight how Mr X helped solve some serious problem which saved a significant amount of money for the company. I could say something like: "Mr X has done exemplary work and merits your attention, and your department is lucky to have someone of his professional calibre." I can use my time to write a personal thank-you email to someone who has helped me, detailing how much their contribution was worth, how involved they were and how proud I was to work alongside them, and copy in all their superiors and the members of the executive committee concerned with the initiative. I can always use my time to go and see the director of human resources to point out some potential talent. In short, I aim to carry out projects that are beneficial for the company, for me and for those who help me by trading their efforts for my time. (Don't forget that time is money!) This technique has always served me well and most of the people who have helped me have, as a result, had more bonuses, more promotions and more success in weathering restructuring plans than the average employee.

The last factor on my list is fear. You could also call it "The Stick", and rebrand the second factor described above as "The Carrot" instead of talking about rewards. Many would call me out for being cynical and my reply would be a firm "Not at all!" We all know that the company environment is harsh, a modern jungle populated with people trying to survive and get ahead. You are competing against other people, some competent, others less so, some kind-hearted, others fundamentally nasty. It doesn't really matter what they are like, just remember that you are competing.

If a kind-hearted and competent person can help you with a project, you should make sure this person is on your side. Sometimes people aren't motivated by the money, might be feeling down, can't see the point of your brilliant project, throw in the towel halfway through, or just don't like you or have a negative view of you. When this happens, fear can help you break the deadlock to your advantage. If this person is competing against a nasty incompetent (or a nasty competent, or anyone else), make them understand that you are offering them the opportunity to score points and impress. You are offering them the opportunity to maintain their lead or make up for lost time or rediscover the motivation they lost years ago. If the company is going through a lean period and restructuring is on the table, this person would be an easy target because they are too static. Many people are resigned to their fate and keep their head down while they wait for that phone call or letter from human resources. Remind this person of the current situation, their attitude that makes them a sitting target, their family… And then get them on board. By joining you on your project, they will get out of the firing line, have a better chance of continuing their run in the company and, who knows, maybe they will get a taste for pursuing success too. At the end of the project, don't forget to be proud of your successful project. If the company is being restructured, don't hesitate to indicate to those doing the restructuring that you are working on a high-value project with a group of people who are absolutely essential to its success – and list their names.

Trust, profit and fear: my winning trio for inspiring those around me.

How did I find out about this winning trio? Quite simply through doing the total opposite, because I didn't foster trust, I wasn't making a profit and I was at the mercy of fear. I never managed to do anything very useful, I was a cost burden for my employers and I rarely succeeded in inspiring others to follow me. While my ego tried to hide the truth by putting my lack of success down to being misunderstood and a victim of injustice, other people were quite right not to follow my lead.

When something doesn't work, you have no other choice but to change it.

3.12
Be yourself, but not for too long

You often hear people being exhorted to "Be yourself". But surely that depends on who you are and who you want to be, no?

I am now in my forties and perfectly happy not to be the person I was when I was twenty or thirty. When I was twenty, I was an idiot. Do I want to continue being an idiot? No. At thirty, I was skint. Do I want to continue being skint? No. Every year I learn new things, not just in a professional capacity, but also in my private life and more generally about the world around me. Every year I feel like I have progressed – albeit slowly – along an endless path. Every year I appreciate the progress I have made. As a result, I don't regret being who I was one year ago and I am happy to no longer be that person.

In the professional sphere, it is very dangerous to adhere to the be-yourself mantra, because that way stagnation lies, and that means danger. You should always be learning, progressing, maintaining your lead. You can't just "be yourself" in a company unless you do it deliberately and are prepared to accept the consequences.

On a personal level, life changes us. People you meet, people you lose, those you love and those you detest, those who open your eyes to new things, those who tend to make you regress, those who encourage you, those who disappoint you... All of them contribute to your development. As with everyone else, your experience is unique. You have developed in your own way, questioned some of your inherited convictions, accepted others, and have built a system of values that changes over time.

When you have a set solid set of principles, when you feel comfortable with them, so you aren't frustrated or sad but instead thriving, happy and comfortable with who you are, then your values are sound. If they suit you, hold them dear. If not, change or get rid of whatever it is that is troubling you.

However your values aren't you. They are just a part of you. You can always keep your system of values as it is, if it suits you and makes you happy, but you should continue to learn and progress. Bear in mind that it isn't a good idea to confuse your values with your state of mind, experience and skills. Even if all these factors are connected, each one is nonetheless separate and distinct. A solid set of values, one which you feel in harmony with, can become static because there is no pressing reason for its composition to change. But that doesn't mean you can't evolve while preserving the values that feel right for you. It isn't incompatible, in fact it is quite the opposite.

Humans are social animals and we are all influenced by our environment. We all tend to become a sort of "average" or "mean" of the people that we interact with on a daily basis. Someone who lives in an environment which values enterprise, culture, philosophy and constructive debate will be pushed to change and progress according to a solid set of values. Somebody less lucky, whose environment comprises people who have no grasp of how a company operates, how the economic system works or how to develop projects will have greater difficulties to face. That person will have to reconsider much of their values system as they progress through life, learning how to take risks and questioning their lifestyle. And their progress will be made all the more difficult because they will certainly have to deal with people who will hold them back or try to hold them back with banal remarks such as "You take too many risks", "It will never work", "You need to keep your head down", "Learn to be satisfied with what you have" or "That's not for people like us". If you are in a situation like the one just described, you cannot continue to "be yourself" without risking failure in the key objectives of surviving and succeeding in the workplace. Not only do you need to learn, as we all do, but you also need to change the system of values that you have been nurturing probably since you were very young.

For some, being oneself involves doing and saying what you want, in effect it means having rights. For my part, I have never known a single person of this type achieve any real measure of success. Many survive, but mostly in some insignificant role or obscure corner of the office building. A company is a group of people who, despite their differences, must work together to generate profits. For that to work, the company needs to be organized, have rules and apply strategies, all of which are incompatible with the notion of "doing what you want" unless of course what you want is to be part of an organization which has rules and applies strategies.

Equally, freedom of expression is fundamental and everyone should have the right to express an idea, a suggestion or a concern. In the workplace, what you say needs to be constructive. Criticizing gratuitously is damaging. Criticizing is easy. Denigrating is easy. Doing is difficult. Building is difficult. Progressing is difficult. Criticism is helpful when it demonstrates that, for example, an idea is dangerous, but it also needs to offer practical and viable solutions. What is said must not be offensive, instead it must be based on facts, be ethical and respect the person whose idea is being criticized.

Also, if everybody has rights, then it goes that everybody has duties. In the workplace your principal duty is to contribute to the company's success.

Lastly, if after all these years you have learnt nothing, have failed to progress in either your personal or professional life, and have remained in the same job without changing a thing, then watch out! Perhaps you have tried to "be yourself" overly long. Don't forget that stagnating in the short and medium terms is a risk for your survival and eliminates almost all your chances of achieving success.

3.13
Be a good marketing product

Are you familiar with the term "marketing mix"? It is an approach to marketing which focuses on the fundamental constituents of a product, which are the item itself (or service), how much it sells for, the communications used to market it, and how it is distributed. It is often summarized as: product, price, place and promotion.

Whether you like it or not, you are a service in the job market. The service you provide involves your skills, your experience and your personality. Your salary is your price. If your price is greater than the money you actually generate, either in turnover or savings, you are a cost. If your price is clearly lower than what you cost, you are a profitable investment. If your price is very much lower than what you cost, you are an excellent investment and it might be time to raise your price a little without losing your status as an excellent investment.

Your distribution network is the way you sell yourself. Do you look for work by replying to job adverts or do people spontaneously offer you opportunities? For as long as I was a cost, my strategy for finding work involved replying to job adverts and I had to send out an incredible number of applications before finding a company that was willing to take me on. Once I became a profitable investment and my results became common knowledge in the market, I no longer had to send out job applications at all. Now people contact me directly, often on the recommendation of a common acquaintance, and offer me opportunities. I really used to struggle to get a company to say "Yes". Now I just say "No thanks" more often than not. What's even better is that, when times are hard and opportunities for employment become scarcer, the number of job opportunities for me are increasing. When you think about it, it is logical. When times are good and money is flowing freely, you can easily cover costs. When times become hard and money gets scarcer, you have to reduce your outgoings and find new sources of income or savings.

Communication is a fundamental factor and I quickly realized its importance, even though for many years my own communication was poor, counter-productive even.

Let me give you a simple example involving chocolate. (Who doesn't like chocolate?)

Imagine you are in a shop which has two packets of chocolate cake. One looks ordinary, even a bit sad, with just the words Chocolate Cake on the box and it costs $3. The other looks magnificent, with a photo showing a soft chocolate centre under a caption saying Delicious cake with the incredible flavour of chocolate! and it costs $5. A lot of people buy the second cake because it is more tempting. And yet the second one isn't a chocolate cake, it just has the flavour – albeit "incredible" – of chocolate. Worse, it turns out that it doesn't taste as good as the first one and costs $2 more. The moral of the story is simple: we tend to judge by appearance rather than use our reason. But it is too late, the fancy packet containing a mediocre product got the sale. The other packet, the one containing the good cake, got left on the shelf, unsold. If there are so many mediocre employees in the workplace, it is partly because many people responsible for hiring them get fooled by the candidates who are not necessarily competent but have mastered the art of communicating and presenting themselves. Twenty years ago I suffered from this very same problem. Opportunities regularly passed me by, whereas less competent people were managing to do better.

Now, imagine that you have heard about a delicious cake being sold in a shop at No. 46 Somewhere Street. You decide that you need to try this famous phenomenon of the pastry world, regardless of its packaging. Indeed, regardless of its packaging because its reputation has done the work. Word of mouth is a powerful tool and certainly the best type of publicity. All you have to do is be successful in your job and get tangible, quantifiable results, which you broadcast to your colleagues inside and outside the company. Word of mouth does the rest. We'll come back to the importance of communications later in the book. Just be aware that word of mouth takes time and reputations take many long years to establish. Also be aware that it only takes a few moments to ruin a reputation, so you should take the utmost care of yours.

I have never liked the idea of being a product in the market, like a yoghurt, a vacuum cleaner or a tray of raw meat. My ego didn't want to accept this truth and that was the case for many years. The reality of my situation was nevertheless inescapable, and my ignoring it meant that I didn't get the results. I had to accept the truth. It was a fantastic lesson in humility which enabled me to see life and my part in it from another viewpoint, that is to say with my eyes wide open to the reality of a world even more cynical than I would have ever dared imagine. Reading Marcus Aurelius helped getting me over this hurdle. The writings of great leaders can be very effective in bringing inflated egos back to earth and making them see sense.

Once you are an employee, a consultant or a professional, that is to say once you rely on somebody to fund your lifestyle and your existence, you are a product or a service.

It is a harsh but unavoidable rule. It is up to you to accept it, to put it to good use, and to make sure that you are maintaining a good "marketing mix".

4
Planning Instead of Executing

Once you have become aware of your environment and no longer harbour illusions about your company, once you have taken on board the notions and soft skills mentioned in the preceding chapters, it is time for you to take action.

A company is generally home to two categories of employee: those who plan and those who execute.

Less charitable minds might say there are those who think and those who follow orders. I don't agree with this assessment, and what I see daily in the workplace contradicts this harsh view, too. Anyone who executes orders without thinking ends up doing very little, while those who think without knowing how to perform a task are often wrong. The thinker who doesn't know how to accomplish tasks more often causes damage to a company than generates profit.

Many of you reading this are executing or started out by executing. Executing positions, that is to say work which involves repeating an algorithm or following an established process, offer no leeway for implementing new ideas or modifying how you go about a task. They are however useful when you are starting out. They allow you to understand the situation in the field and the operational issues, thus raising your awareness of a fundamental reality.

Many thinkers never leave their ivory towers and prefer to view the world through figures and charts. Their ideas and decisions are often out of sync with the situation in the field, rarely produce the intended results, and often complicate the lives of the employees on the ground instead of improving them. And when something works well, thinkers can't just leave it alone because they need to show the world that they exist and are active. With such a mindset producing ineffective, useless and sometimes downright stupid projects, it is understandable that many companies gradually turn into bureaucracies whose sole aim seems to be to increase their chances of triggering a crisis.

An executing position is a useful teacher. The problem with executing positions is that those who occupy them tend to stagnate. And as we've already seen, stagnation means danger. If you already occupy a planning position, then you should aim to move to a position where you can achieve even more. If you are currently in an executing position, you need to move to a planning position.

Executing positions aren't just about being a worker. Most doctors and physicians execute repetitive protocols (e.g. listen to the patient, take their temperature, look in their mouth, identify where it hurts) and probably prescribe the same treatment several times a day. Many engineers interpret the results of their analyses in a repetitive way. Many technicians repeat the exact same checks and controls. Many insurance underwriters draw up contracts with the selfsame clauses over and over again during their careers. Executing positions such as these are undoubtedly under threat from the rapid progress being made in artificial intelligence. Trading transactions, the analysis of geological surveys, X-rays and MRI scans, engineering projects, industrial maintenance and many other tasks undertaken by high-level specialists are relying increasingly on artificial intelligence and some are even being automated. Many manual jobs have been replaced by machines. Many engineers and other high-level specialists will be gradually replaced by software, unless of course they progress and use software applications as tools for increasing their professional skills.

In order to survive the great changes occurring in technology and business models, the rise in robotics and artificial intelligence, the increase in international competition, and the vagaries of the current economic situation, you need to progress from executing projects and start planning them. That is the subject of this chapter.

First of all, a project needs to satisfy the expectations of the greatest number of people, which is why we shall be going over the goals of the main stakeholder categories in a company (operational employees, middle managers, directors). Next, we shall look at how to identify opportunities for creating and achieving projects. And lastly, we shall see how to take advantage of your results so you don't just survive but start achieving success.

4.1
Understand the goals of the executive management

The higher up you are in the hierarchy, the closer you get to the shareholders who are after one thing only: more profits to increase their dividends and the price of their shares.

When a company is in crisis, before even considering turning a profit, it must stop haemorrhaging money and try to stabilize its finances. Such crises within a company are often the result of reversals in the economic situation, the arrival of a new technology or technique, or perhaps a business model which has become obsolete. Many firms owned partially or wholly by government are also in a similar situation, regardless of their country of registration. For these kinds of companies, the shareholders (including the government) aim foremost to reduce losses and at least return it to some kind of stable footing. Profit for them is often but a dream that they can rarely countenance in the short and medium terms. Reviews to restructure departments, services, workforces, market positions and more are all priorities for such enterprises – and their shareholders want concrete results.

The shareholders own the company. They appoint and dismiss the directors, who in turn appoint and dismiss the middle managers, who in turn appoint and dismiss the employees.

In every case, if you contribute to doing as much or more with less, to making additional sales, to increasing margins, to reducing losses or to solving problems that weigh heavily on the company, then you are contributing to enhancing the profitability of the company and thus to satisfying its shareholders. That will satisfy your boss, your boss's boss, and the next boss up and so on. In every case, that is good for you.

4.2 Understand the goals of middle management

Middle management is fundamentally separated from the shareholders by the executive management, which it fears. Not only does executive management pass pressure from the shareholders on to middle management, it can also be the source of convoluted ideas that the middle managers then have to implement in order to survive. In the latter case, middle management often has to mobilize salaried employees who are neither convinced nor motivated by these ideas.

Middle management is the layer in the hierarchy which has to deal with disgruntled customers and demotivated or absent employees, draft all sorts of reports for the executive management, and stimulate the sales of products customers aren't interested in... In short, middle managers have to put up with a lot, and often for salaries which are much lower than those of the executive management.

Middle management abounds with attractive positions and once you yourself are a middle manager, you will discover opportunities for promotion. On the other hand, middle managers who want to rise to the top find that there is a glass ceiling they cannot breach. They can only develop their careers horizontally, that is to say they can access other positions but at the same level in the hierarchy that they already occupy, unless they change company. If they choose to follow that path, they could progress to an executive management position but most of the time they would have to move to a smaller company.

When you are a member of middle management and report to an executive manager, your objectives are simple and often focus on generating profit or at the very least minimizing losses from one year to the next.

Things aren't so simple when you are a member of middle management and report to another middle manager or have to supervise operational employees. You are obviously expected to contribute to making profits (reducing losses), sometimes in the form of cost goals which might turn out to be unrealistic. You also have to achieve this while dealing with all the other issues described earlier in this chapter: producing reports, managing schedules, and dealing with absent or demotivated employees, disgruntled customers, computer-related problems, complaints, exceptional situations that fall outside the scope of established procedure, last-minute emergencies, and the competition coming from other middle managers (which is much tougher than what the executives experience).

Do you report to a middle manager? Not only do you have to contribute to the financial objectives of your boss, you also have to give him or her support, loyalty and the comfort of knowing they can count on you day in day out in the pursuit of achieving their own goals.

4.3
Understand the expectations of operational employees

Operational employees are the "executors" who produce, maintain, sell or manage daily business... under the supervision of middle management.

There are often asked to do more, sometimes much more, with increasingly demanding targets and constraints. They are exhorted to produce more and faster, sell more and faster, sell unsellable products and services, carry out maintenance faster...

They are also the first to suffer in restructuring plans and the renegotiation of contracts. And they are also the ones who see bosses come and go, which either changes nothing in their daily life or results in changes that often only complicate their work. If a boss is competent, good, and changes things in a positive way, they won't be in the position for very long before getting promoted or tempted away by the competition.

Operational employees often start out motivated but over time they get worn down by their situation, by the lack of recognition and promotion from their hierarchy despite their best efforts.

Operational employees usually report to a middle manager. If they are to survive, they need to perform their tasks properly. They need to contribute to the success and comfort of the middle manager who supervises them, while remaining aware that their boss will rarely show them gratitude. Which is understandable on the part of the boss, because it is in their interest to hinder the promotion or departure of an employee who contributes efficiently to their own results and provides them with very useful support.

4.4
Operational position: a long-term danger that needs to be turned into an opportunity

It should now be clear in your mind that an operational position becomes a dangerous situation over time. That doesn't mean that you can't be anything other than an operational employee, even if many do indeed believe that is the case and remain so throughout their lives.

To remain safe in an operational position usually means never having to deal with competition (new generations, foreign competition, new technologies), crises, restructuring plans, bad bosses... And for a salary which at best can offer you a few extras and a week or two in the sun once all the basic bills have been paid.

Remaining in an operational position is a bit like playing Russian roulette because, the longer the game lasts, the fewer empty chambers there are in the barrel. And there is also the boredom which can come from the routine, the risk of gradually losing all self-esteem, and the feeling of having achieved nothing in life, apart from bringing up children in the hope they will do better than you.

When you hear the term "operational position", the image that often springs to mind is of a worker, a maintenance technician, a ticket clerk or some similar job. But then you would be forgetting that many operational positions can be middle-management ones, in particular in departments involved in administrating, auditing, etc. And much less attention is paid to middle-manager unemployment than it is to workers losing their jobs.

An employee in an operational position will struggle to cross over and join those who organize, enhance and optimize. In short, they must bring value to the company not through executing tasks but by making proposals and nurturing specific projects. This can only mean one thing: stop being passive, start taking the initiative.

4.5
Be attentive to your company and its problems

Before taking the initiative, you need to find a suitable opportunity to exploit. For my part, I have never known a company that doesn't have a problem or, to put it another way, I have never come across a company that doesn't conceal an opportunity. Are you concerned about missing an opportunity or not having one at all? Don't worry, you might miss one but there will be a dozen more to come.

First of all, look around you, in your office, your department and your division. What are the recurrent, daily problems? What do you and your colleagues waste your time on? What does the company lose money on? If you have to deal with customers, what annoys them or makes them hesitate in completing the purchase? If you have to deal with suppliers, what causes delays, compliance problems and other issues? Talk to your colleagues to get a better idea of the problem and find out how it impacts them. How much time do they spend dealing with this problem?

Next, try to ascertain any concerns or worries that your superiors might have involving your department or division. In your part of the company (department, division, unit, shop, etc.) are the results stalling or the costs rocketing? Do other departments or third parties (customers, suppliers, service providers) file complaints involving your department? What would your hierarchy like to improve about your department, its role and future assignments? How would they like to see it develop? Whenever you come into contact with senior executives, talk to them about it. If they aren't very accessible, obtain information from those close to them or have a chat with your human resources manager during your annual evaluation. Try, too, to get your hands on the business reports which focus on your department so you can study how the indicators change.

Read the company's annual report, if they publish one. Look at the company's financial health and compare it to the performance of its competitors. Start reading business-to-business publications, and all the opinions, analyses and comments you can find on the Web. If other companies are doing things differently and getting better results, take inspiration from their experiences to develop new ideas.

See what your customers think. Do they think the products are good but expensive? If the company's costs are high, any idea to optimize production in order to bring down the retail price is worth looking into.

You need to be attentive, all the time. You need to be a good observer, on the alert for the slightest signal that might indicate an opportunity (or a danger). Develop an information-gathering network which includes your colleagues in the company's various departments and entities, members of the executive committee or people close to them, the company's customers and partners, reports, resources on the internet...

There will be multiple problems to solve. It is up to you to filter out the poor options, and identify those problems that are feasible for you, that you can work on to demonstrate your potential, that you can turn into opportunities.

Never forget that the problem – and thus the opportunity – you are looking for could be right under your nose.

4.6
Foster opportunities and bring them to fruition

Once you have identified an opportunity, you need to reassure yourself of its chances of success before you commit to it and ask your hierarchy for approval. If you don't thoroughly think it through before you start, you increase your chances of failure considerably. And failures will undermine your credibility and tarnish your reputation.

Keep your thoughts to yourself while you are assessing the opportunity. Don't talk about it to anybody. News spreads fast in the workplace. Leaks are common so always keep in mind that an ill-intentioned person might get wind of your projects and try to sabotage or appropriate them. Don't forget that you are in a jungle, a competitive environment populated with as many unscrupulous individuals as principled ones, and they are all playing the success game.

Assess the problem and convert it into cash. For example, estimate how much time is wasted per day and per person. Multiply that by the number of people concerned and the number of working days per year (don't count weekends and holidays). Without investing much time and energy, you have just estimated the number of hours the problem gobbles up every year. Make your approach more reliable – and thus more credible in the eyes of the decision makers – by obtaining the average amount of time your colleagues spend on the issue every day. This can be done informally, for example over lunch or during a coffee break. If your colleagues are paid a similar wage to you, multiply the wasted hours by your hourly rate. This hourly rate should be the gross rate (before the deduction of tax and other contributions) of your salary plus whatever else you cost the company. You can find estimations on the internet or from your human resources manager. By multiplying the number of wasted hours per year by the average hourly rate, you will be able to estimate the cost of the problem. Keep a copy of your calculations and sources safe for future reference. Next look at how much time you will need to solve the problem and put a figure on it using your hourly rate. If you need reinforcements to put together a small team, add their time to your estimate. Include any expenses relating to tangibles and outside help (although use in-house resources wherever possible). The result is a cost-benefit analysis of the opportunity. If the cost is considerably less than the value of the potential benefit, that is excellent news for you.

Next think about the possible solutions. Are they feasible? Which one is the simplest and quickest to implement? How do you implement it? What resources will you need? How much time will you need? What are the risks and counter-arguments, and how do you overcome them? If the plan fails, what will the company lose?

Once you feel at home with your idea, the plan and the potential financial rewards, it is time to get the green light for implementing it. While you are doing this, make sure you are recognized as its legitimate supervisor. It is likely that you will never be 100% sure of success. But once you have gone through it all and you still estimate that you can expect an 80% chance of success, and that your intuition supports your analysis, then go for it.

Don't start by going to see your immediate superior and telling him or her about the project. For a start, they might steal your idea. They could also let you drive the project, leave you to shoulder the risks and carry out the hard work, and then claim all the glory by falsely asserting that it was their idea, that they encouraged you, that they guided or supervised you... They could even inflate their own results without you knowing and even obtain a bonus or a promotion on the back of your good work. Never go to your direct superior first unless they are a senior executive.

Talk about the problem (and its associated figures) with your boss's boss or, if possible, someone even higher up the hierarchy. Ask them, for example in the lift or at the coffee machine, if they are interested in making savings for the company. Any normal individual will obviously say "Yes". Tell them that you have identified an additional cost of approximately X dollars (your estimate) and think you know how to reduce the problem. Ask them again if they are interested. They will almost certainly say "Yes" again. If this is indeed the case, offer to describe your proposal in writing and present it to them in a few weeks once you've gone through it with your direct manager. If you manage to talk to someone higher up, ask them the same questions as if they were your direct manager's boss. The point is making sure that your direct manager's superiors are aware of the fact that it is your idea, your project and not anyone else's. It is the best way to retain the ownership of your idea.

Now it is time to work discreetly on your project. Make a slide show and summarize the key points in the following order: the current problem and what it costs, the suggested solution and how much it costs, the expected savings, and the schedule for implementing the solution. Call on your direct superior and present your project using the slide show. Carefully observe their reaction.

If they subscribe to your idea and agree to give you their green light, thank them and reassure them in their decision by explaining that you will do your utmost to ensure the success of the project. Mention too that your immediate superior's boss, or a senior executive, was interested in the idea (not the project) and suggested that you discuss the project (and not the idea) with your immediate superior, not just to get their opinion, but also to benefit from their experience and expert eye (even if your immediate superior possesses neither). Next, organize a meeting with your immediate superior, their manager and a more senior executive if possible. If the project is a good one it will almost certainly get approval, and you will then be able to take action with the backing of your superiors. They might have doubts, which is normal, but if the worst that can come of it is wasting a little of your time, how can they say "No"?

Don't forget that your senior manager might well feel threatened by your immediate superior. And in turn, your senior manager might constitute a threat to the executive above them. Your senior manager will be delighted to discover that they can count on you to thwart any attacks coming from their immediate subordinate (your boss). Managers are often focused on promotion and power, and this can motivate them to use all their guile and deception to discredit their immediate superior in the hope of replacing them one day (preferably sooner rather than later).

Not only will you ensure ownership of your project, you will also get the credit if it is successful. You will also catch the eye of your superiors, who often lack enterprising, value-creating people like you that they can rely on to help them achieve their annual performance targets.

Hang on a minute, what if your boss says "No"? Well, you need to determine what the best option is. If your immediate superior does indeed refuse, and your relations with them are good, you should tell them about your senior manager's interest in the project. If on the other hand you are at war with your boss, go and see your senior manager to share the bad news and your disappointment. Ultimately, how you choose to deal with a refusal is up to you, but make sure you take into account the context and listen to your intuition. Whatever you decide, don't throw in the towel too quickly. Instead, try to understand why your manager refused. Talk to them about their decision and figure out what motivated them to say "No". In some cases, objections can be overcome by revising your plan and providing solutions to what could well be legitimate concerns. Finding those solutions will be your job. In other cases their reasons might be totally unfounded, perhaps because they are lazy, because they don't want to let a subordinate cast a shadow on them, or even because they want to keep a low profile! If their reasons really are so petty and trivial, then you will be more than justified in going to see your senior manager about their refusal.

In certain cases you can quickly secure the necessary approval for pursuing your project in, for example, meetings that include your senior manager and perhaps other managers of their rank or higher. If one of the items on the agenda or in the discussions concerns the company's struggle to make savings, speak up once everybody else has had their say. Outline the problem you have identified and how much it costs the company annually. Point out that even if addressing the problem won't reverse the fortunes of the company on its own, it will nevertheless be a positive contribution. Ask the chairman of the meeting if, in principle, they are interested and offer to study the problem in greater detail and, if a simple, inexpensive solution exists, you will submit it to them in the coming weeks. You'll have a good chance of getting your green light and, as a result, the authority for launching your project, at the very least the feasibility study.

For some people, in particular non-managerial employees who are not well-known to their superiors, this type of approach can be somewhat difficult to pull off. A possible solution would be to speak to a human resources manager about your desire to take on more responsibilities, and quickly outline (without going into the details) the expenses or wastage that the company could avoid, that cost it dear every year (you could mention some estimates) and that you could mitigate if you were given the opportunity to do so. If you have the nerve, why not knock on the door of a top-level manager and use the five minutes they give you to outline your ideas and state your desire to develop your career?

4.7
Guiding a project to fruition

Once you have obtained the green light, you need to carry out your project in accordance with four crucial phases: initiation and planning, cost analysis, action plan, monitoring.

Project Initiation and Planning

First of all, if you can't manage your project on your own then you will need to put together a team. Keep its members to a minimum. It is much easier to manage a situation involving four people rather than thirty. You will also reduce the risk of being double-crossed or betrayed if your team is small. Another point in favour of operating with a skeleton crew is it is cheaper to run. And of course, if the project is successful, the rewards will go to a minimal number of people, thus optimizing the value of each individual share.

Try to create a team with people you know or who have a good reputation both in their technical abilities and their social skills. You need to be able to rely on competent and honest colleagues. Explain to them the problem, how much it costs the company, your project, the chosen solution and the expected benefits, and don't forget to mention that your superiors have given you the green light. In short, sell them the project and how it is an opportunity to add value to the company and a chance to get noticed by the executive management.

Once you have achieved this step, define the project schedule and allocate the tasks to each member of the team. Look carefully at each task with the experts in your team. What result do you expect to gain from each individual task? In what form? According to what time frame? If possible, check with the relevant expert on how they intend to proceed. If they have some doubts, what solution can they propose? If another member of the team has to work with this expert or build upon the results that they are expected to produce, make sure that they communicate with each other, that they agree on the deliverables and expectations, and that neither of them will encounter a nasty surprise that could delay or compromise the project. Make sure, too, that none of the team has a comprehensive overview of the project because you might get pushed aside...

If some tasks turn out to be longer or more complex than expected, add extra time to your schedule. And always add a generous margin for unexpected events. I usually add two or three months to a project which is normally expected to take a year. This gives me time to sort out any problems without getting flustered and ensures that I'm not seen as unreliable in the eyes of the top-level management when it comes to meeting deadlines.

Once the tasks have been clearly defined and allocated, and the team is coordinated and committed to the deadlines, each expert can get to work. Establish milestones with each team member so you can check the tasks are progressing and that they comply with your expectations. Above all, don't wait until the end of a task before checking on it because you might get a nasty surprise, and experience major delays if the completed work does not meet your expectations and has to be done again from start to finish. You also risk demotivating the team responsible for the task and they might abruptly throw in the towel, which is not an option for you.

If your project involves sales outlets, production facilities or other sites, don't just sit in your office all day, but go and see what is happening on the ground. Chat with the people involved, from the highest manager to the lowliest worker. Solutions are often to be found at or near the bottom of the ladder, in places where staff don't deal with computer spreadsheets but instead with customers and products. Highlight this approach when you are making your presentation to senior management. You will show them that you are prepared to get your hands dirty in pursuit of practical solutions. They will be impressed.

Cost Analysis

We will develop this aspect further a little later in the book.

This phase of the project is a fundamental one because it justifies in economic terms your idea and the resulting action plan. This is often the moment when others try to prevent you from carrying out your project by questioning or casting doubt on your figures. There is a reason for this: when you highlight a problem, you are also highlighting the people who caused it or failed to resolve it. Albert Einstein was right when he said that you should never count on the person who created the problem to solve it...

Your first choice should always be to use your company's own data: accounting data, production data, sales data, quality assurance data, health and safety data, human resources data, and so on. That way your sources will carry more weight and will be less vulnerable to criticism. For example, if you use the production department's data, anybody who questions the reliability of your figures will also be casting doubt on the production management's ability to produce reliable figures, and that could turn out to be a foolish move politically. If your analysis contains in-house accounting data, marketing data, production data and sales data, any belligerent colleague who attacks your figures also risks turning a large number of their colleagues against them, so it is unlikely to happen. Additionally, senior management will be delighted to see its departments working as a team and will probably view your figures as trustworthy because they are drawn directly from company resources.

Check your figures carefully. How did you work them out? What do they include? Imagine that you observe a significant reduction in sales at a regional franchise outlet from looking at the sales data, and that marketing studies indicate a deepening crisis in purchasing power in the region. You could conclude that prices are too high and need to be lowered. However it could be the case that certain outlets were closed for two months to allow time for renovation works... Now imagine that you talked to the management about your observations, that sales are down because of a significant fall in disposable income in the region. And then suddenly someone says that the situation is perfectly normal because the sales outlets in the region are closed for renovation… In less than a minute, public humiliation will reduce your reputation to tatters for the foreseeable future.

It is essential, then, to understand how the figures you are using were calculated from start to finish. You also need to compare them with other figures to reinforce your analysis and ensure its pertinency. You also need to go through your analysis with the experts in your team and reassure yourself that they concur. If they don't, try to understand what is wrong and revise your findings. Don't hesitate to consult other experts who can give you an opinion, one that will give your analysis greater legitimacy.

Understanding your figures is primordial. You also need to be sure that there is general support among your colleagues for your analysis – and its figures – before submitting it to senior management.

Action Plan

Your action plan should be simple, clear, efficient and above all an indisputable source of added value. Similar to the cost analysis, it must enjoy the general support of your colleagues.

By simple and clear, I mean that everybody – experts and non-experts alike – should be able to understand the proposed actions and why they should be implemented. What does each action involve? Who implements it? When, how, and with what?

By efficient, I mean that you don't try to eliminate entirely the problem highlighted by your cost analysis. Instead, adopt the 80/20 rule as a basic principle. If four or five actions can reduce the problem by 70–80%, that's good enough. I have noticed that only a few actions are required in most situations to mitigate a problem considerably. The additional actions required to entirely resolve the problem tend to demand much more effort for very little extra gain. Be efficient and above all don't be a perfectionist chasing a costly ideal.

Although an unquestionable source of added value, actions do nevertheless require time and resources. In other words, each action will cost your company money. Estimate the cost of each action and compare this cost to the expected benefits. If an action is going to require three days' work for two engineers and an investment of $100,000 to save $300,000 per year over five years, it is clearly a worthwhile endeavour and deserves to be undertaken. If on the other hand the combined efforts make savings of $80,000 per year, the action is still profitable but becomes less attractive for a senior manager if they are searching for rapid results. Losing money in the first year, even if its purpose is to make money in subsequent years, is never going to attract much enthusiasm because people nearly always prefer the safety of the present to the uncertainty of the future. Personally, I always make sure that the actions I take on will generate profits of at least 100% (i.e. return twice as much as they cost), and that they do so as soon as they are implemented. I exclude systematically any action with an expected profitability of less than 20%. If an action costs more than it generates in the first twelve months but offers good prospects for the second year, I append it to an action or actions that can immediately generate considerable benefits. Dog owners will recognize this technique as the one they use when their pet refuses to swallow the medicine prescribed by the vet: hide the pill in a tasty morsel and Fido will lap it up! It is the same thing with actions. So remember, maximum profitability as soon as possible.

Some will say that you can't predict the profitability of these kinds of actions. They are undeniably correct and that is why we always speak of "estimates". It is also why we choose actions with the greatest returns on investment because they can afford protection from unexpected events. If, for whatever reason, an action estimated to have an 80% profit margin gets compromised by an unexpected event and the return falls to 15%, it remains nevertheless a profitable endeavour. And it is not every day that you come across an investment offering a 15% return.

Monitoring

Monitoring is an often forgotten but very crucial part of a project. For a start, it is the only way you can tell if your actions were properly implemented. And it enables you to measure the impacts and added value. Monitoring the results also allows you to log your annual performance, and your aggregate performance which, each year, puts a figure on your contribution to the company in return for your salary.

Your project is an asset, that is to say a source of added value which will "finance" your survival in the company, and also a building block in your success. If you project generates $100,000 per year in savings over three years, that's $100,000 you can put in your annual performance report for the next three years. If you cost your company $80,000 a year, including additional expenses, your employment is more or less a "neutral" cost. If you cost your company $50,000 a year, you are clearly a good return. If you cost $160,000 annually, then your drain on company finances over the next three years will only be $60,000 a year.

Now, if you have three projects underway and they are generating a total of $230,000 per year, then you are definitely a good investment. If you are paid $50,000, it is time you discussed promotions and bonuses, but don't be too greedy because you need to remain a good, not to say excellent investment for the company. For my part, I make sure I bring into the company at least ten times my gross salary every year.

So you need to watch over your asset like a hawk. First of all, make sure that your actions have been properly implemented. Next, in concert with the people who implemented them with you, determine how much money (or time) the actions really did save or generate for the company. Add these results to your logbook of achievements every year.

Make sure that nothing hinders the implementation of your actions, nor their continuation. As soon as a problem presents itself, it is down to you to work with the experts concerned to find a solution. Above all, you mustn't give up on it. Each action you give up on reduces your results, and in turn reduces your chances of survival or success.

Lastly, some actions might not work as expected. Some might turn out to be good ideas on paper only. Others might turn out to be impractical. If nothing can be done to rectify the situation and transform the flawed action into a success, let it go. Don't be scared to admit failure and learn from it. If a couple of actions fail out a total of eight and your plan continues to be highly profitable, your project will still be considered a success. Were you aiming to make $120,000 but in the end it was more like $105,000? Without doubt, you made less than expected but don't lose sight of what matters: you did make money.

4.8
Estimate, document and demonstrate added value in your projections and results

The reliability of your work and your results must be indisputable. In other words, your method and your calculations must never be open to an interpretation that an ill-intentioned person can use against you. You have two weapons in your arsenal to prevent this: diligence and transparency.

Let's deal with diligence first. You should understand very clearly the problem you highlight and the numbers you use, regardless of the source. Use nothing that you do not understand, even if gaining an understanding of it requires a lot more work. Talk to experts in the field, search the Web, read books and professional magazines, and so on. Compare opinions and form your own opinion. Beware of fake experts, and senior managers who owe their position not to success but to how long they have worked in the company. Beware of emotions and second-hand knowledge, and rely instead on facts and figures so that your opinion is as objective as possible. Any demonstration worth its salt should be more convincing than a great speech (show beats tell). And remember, you should first be convinced yourself of the pertinence of your approach before trying to convince others of it.

The traceability of your figures should also be flawless. You should be able to produce the sources of your figures, all of them without exception. You should be able to explain your hypotheses and your calculations. To do this, use information that your audience considers reliable such as your company's data (accounts, sales, production, marketing, human resources), government figures (official statistics, taxes) and so on. When you present information using a spreadsheet, highlight the pathways and formulas that lead from the (meticulously documented) source data to your findings. This allows you to explain every step of your reasoning, even a couple of years after you drafted the document.

How the figures are interpreted is fundamentally important. And yet figures often give rise to inaccuracies and even mistakes that can cost a company dear. For example, if you look at financial market graphs using short timescales you might observe that certain stocks are experiencing meteoric rises of 30%. On the other hand, when you extend the period of the graph, you discover the same stock lost 30% in the previous year and 45% over the last three years... You should be objective in your analyses and observe the event in question over an extended period.

Doing this will highlight several key factors to include in your analysis. For a start, you will be able to observe a trend. Is it bearish (falling), flat (stagnating) or bullish (rising)? Next, are there any observable cycles and recurring trends? And if there are sudden jumps and drops, what caused them? Everything should have a simple explanation: "Why does the market increase (or decrease) every ten years?" "What causes business to dip and rise in eight-year cycles?" "Why did sales suddenly fall off a cliff in 2017?" Figures should be based on solid argument and common sense. So be meticulous in your analysis before considering any course of action.

If your aim is to reduce, for example, absenteeism in the workplace, you will probably observe peaks that correlate with seasonal flu epidemics and Monday mornings. You might observe considerable discrepancies during, for example, the Covid-19 lockdowns. To combat absenteeism, you can rely on numerous possible actions, such as free flu vaccines, stricter hygiene measures, vitamin-enriched food in the company canteen, flexible working hours, or bonuses paid for regular attendance to limit the "Monday effect" (it is the most popular day to be off sick). As for lockdowns, you will have to come up with some creative solutions to deal with urgent problems, stem losses or benefit from the situation. Whatever the case, you will need to isolate the various contributing factors (Covid-19, seasonal flu, absenteeism for family reasons, etc.). If you don't, you risk having your analysis picked apart by someone who understands the figures and is ready to cast doubt on them in public.

If Monday absenteeism accounts for 3% of the workforce, you can determine how much it costs the company from their salaries or from the associated loss of production. If flexible working hours can reduce the problem to 0.8%, you will easily be able to calculate the benefits of your action every year and add that to your performance report. Of course you won't be able to include in your calculations the Mondays during the covid-19 lockdowns when absenteeism was close to 100%...

4.9
Praise colleagues and show leadership

Once you have completed your project and it is running smoothly, don't forget to show your gratitude to your team and everybody else who has helped you.

Ideally you should organize a review meeting with senior management during which you can present the results your team has achieved. Prepare a final slide which mentions the names and departments of all those involved.

Send them an email to thank them for their contributions. Explain what the project achieved, copy in their superiors, at least their immediate and senior managers, and take the opportunity to thank them for their support (even if they didn't provide any).

Call on the department managers concerned and thank them for their support on this project (once again, even if they didn't provide any) and for allowing you to call on the expertise of their subordinates. Be generous with your compliments and point out that having their subordinate at your side was a decisive factor in the project's success. Keep these thank-you sessions to a few minutes only.

You could also ask for a brief interview with the human resources manager. First, present a summary of the project and the results achieved. Then present the team members who helped you. They will be delighted to be pointed in the direction of these worthy employees who are demonstrating potential, and you will impress them with your ability to bring useful projects to a successful conclusion. You will impress them with your leadership qualities too.

You will gain enormously from taking the time to praise the work of all the contributors to your project.

You will bolster your own self-respect. You have achieved something for the company and, consequently, contributed to its longevity. You did it together with your team. You don't appropriate their work but instead bring them gratitude, recognition and visibility. You increase your chances of survival and success, as well as theirs.

You will improve your visibility in the firm. The management will notice you, know what you have done and how you did it. The human resources manager, your colleagues and their managers will notice you too. And don't forget that word will get around, and as a result a certain number of your colleagues will ensure your promotion.

You will enjoy greater support. Colleagues who put their trust in you won't regret that they did. Without a doubt you will be able to count on them again for your next project. Each project you bring to fruition will reinforce your credibility in the eyes of the management. You will accumulate more supporters, which will incidentally reduce the number of your detractors. The latter will now think twice, even thrice before attacking you. Indeed, it is a bad strategy to attack someone who is perceived to be credible because you risk damaging your own reputation.

You will feel more at ease. Your manager will gradually lose their hold over you. Your results will be common knowledge. It will be hard for them to filter the information or to appropriate the ownership of your work. They will just have to put up with you.

Taking the time to thank and acknowledge others is a powerful communications tool that you should never overlook, especially since it only creates winners... the biggest of them being yourself.

4.10
Take on more tasks, list your achievements, and highlight them in interviews with your superiors, your HR manager and other companies

One success isn't enough to make you a star. You are going to need more, and regularly.

Two or three projects per year is a good target. By that I mean two or three projects per year that deliver results. In a given year you might supervise five projects. Of these, two might deliver their results in the year, two in the following year and the fifth in a couple of years' time. If you undertake too many projects at once, you risk spreading yourself too thinly and this will increase your chances of failure. For most of us, projects run concurrently with everyday tasks. In other words, they are extra work. It is therefore essential to ensure that your projects are given every chance of success and that your efforts to achieve them do not interfere with your everyday work. It is better to have a handful of good projects that are achievable and add value than a vast array of initiatives with uncertain outcomes. Target your efforts with accuracy.

Every year make sure that your regular work, that is to say the work you were initially employed for, is done properly and that you achieve your objectives. Make sure you are able to demonstrate this when somebody questions your diligence. Keep your performance assessments and the associated information somewhere safe where you can find them.

In addition, list all the projects you have undertaken and the value they created. Specify the year, the description of the project and the value generated in dollars. Every year the value created will, in addition to your regular work, raise your profile. You will no longer talk to your superiors and human resources about all the hard work you have done, but about the cash you have generated. You will have become a serious player. You will be a totally different profile, less and less of a financial burden, and one day you will bring in at least as much as you cost. When that happens, you will start being an interesting investment for the company.

If ever you decide to move to another company, perhaps for a more interesting job with better pay, this list of achievements will be very useful and will help you stand out from the other applicants. Not only will you be able to demonstrate your technical competency, you will also be able to show that you can add value to the company by improving and optimizing its processes, services, products, and so on. You will no longer be asking for a job but offering the company an investment opportunity.

What investment? You, obviously!

5
Stay Well Ahead of the Rest of the Field

5.1
Inertia is the worst risk of all

So what is the best way to stagnate and make yourself vulnerable in the workplace? By doing nothing, never changing and just waiting.

We have already looked at the slow-burning risks which can affect you, such as ambitious younger generations, international competition, new techniques, technological progress, fashions, economic crises, mergers and acquisitions... And of course the petty manager who wants to see your head delivered to him on a plate.

In the face of all these risks, you need to take action. Take action by developing your professional mindset. Take action by developing your human capital, that is to say by learning and nurturing professional skills. Like a saver who puts money aside every month, you should learn a little more every month to increase your knowledge, your abilities and your performance. Invest in yourself. Take action by creating value for your company, that is to say by creating new revenue streams or making savings through projects that you undertake alongside your primary tasks. But also take action to ensure that your efforts bear fruit.

You are a professional in your field, working for a salary. You aren't a volunteer. It is normal for you to have a financial interest in the revenues and savings generated by the projects you have guided to fruition, especially since your doing this turns you into an investment for the company. Never be too impatient nor too greedy. Never forget that you should bring in (much) more than you cost, and you need to do this on a regular basis.

Imagine, for example, that your salary amounts to $60,000 a year. The first project you bring to fruition enables the company to save $30,000 a year. The following year your second project generates an additional $10,000 in savings per year. In the third year another project results in a windfall of $80,000 for the company. By now you have generated $190,000 for a cost of

$180,000. You aren't an investment for the company quite yet, but more of a neutral factor because you bring in about as much as you cost. In addition, your projects were undertaken in parallel with your main brief, in other words they are initiatives that you have guided to success. It isn't unreasonable then to envisage a net annual raise of at least 5% of the annual savings generated by your projects, and the allocation of wider responsibilities... So if you have generated a total of $190,000 over three years, thus an average of $63,000 a year, it is relatively easy to justify a raise of $3,000 a year.

Maybe your company won't agree to your request for a raise. Does this mean your efforts were made in vain? Of course not! If this happens, you still have options as to what action to take. You could make an appointment with the director of human resources or your senior manager for the purpose of explaining, backed up with the figures, that your request for a raise or wider responsibilities, or both, is more than reasonable. If your endeavours still fall flat it doesn't really matter, and your disappointment shouldn't stop you. Perhaps it is just time for a change of scenery. You could apply for similar positions in other companies. By highlighting your results and their attendant figures, you would stand out from the job-seeking crowd and could even apply for jobs that are a rung above your current position in the hierarchy, thus advancing your career. Do not remain static in a company that does not reward your efforts over time. You need to be in a win-win mindset.

Excellent opportunities could be just round the corner, but also in a faraway place. If you are currently working in a major city, perhaps you should consider a job in the provinces with greater responsibilities, a pleasant lifestyle and environment, and a lower salary but with more purchasing power. Positions of this type can be an excellent professional springboard, regardless of whether you stay in the provinces or not.

If you have a proven track record, why not take your chances in another country? You could develop your skills, perhaps learn a new language, discover a new culture and acquire new expertise while enjoying better living conditions and a more comfortable salary. Our planet isn't that big and many companies, even the medium-sized ones, are looking to develop internationally. They will need employees who are ready and willing to follow them in such adventures. Whether you are an engineer, a technician or skilled worker, a head chef, a craftsman, an economist or a lawyer, working abroad can be an excellent opportunity, especially if you can negotiate a contract that takes into account your expatriation. Some countries will offer you exceptional conditions in order to benefit from your expertise, which might be common in your home country but rarer elsewhere in the world. What is inaccessible today might be accessible tomorrow, if you are prepared to move...

5.2
Accumulate tasks that generate value and become an expert

A single project brought to fruition will rarely bring you stability and success. You need to accumulate successful projects and keep doing so over time. You need determination and stamina.

Unless your job is to manage projects full time, you are required, like me, to manage general and often routine business on a daily basis. This means that any projects you take on have to be managed alongside the day-to-day stuff, so freeing up time is a critical consideration if you want to bring them to fruition. For my part I only take on a few projects each year, often two or three, in order to maximize my chances of success.

Everyday duties must be taken seriously and executed in a professional manner. If you have trouble managing your general duties, adding special projects to your workload is probably a bad idea. Projects are a plus. They are not something the company requires of you to fulfil the terms of your employment contract. Projects are initiatives that you undertake in addition to your duties. You will find it hard to be taken seriously by your superiors if you aren't good at the job you were hired for, and it will reduce your chances of launching and running special projects in the company.

If you perform your everyday duties efficiently and also undertake successful projects, you are a winner! You will become a real expert and be recognized as such. You won't be one of those self-proclaimed experts but a real master of your trade, recognized by your peers, your superiors and your profession. You will not only be in total control of your everyday work, but you will also be able to optimize it, improve it, make it more efficient, and deliver real added value. Your results will make of you an expert, not your words nor your promises.

And of course, the more projects you guide to success, the more results you will accumulate and the more established becomes your status as an expert. If you lack self-confidence, your results can only bolster the trust you have in your abilities. If you suffer from the much-talked-about impostor syndrome, your results will be your best therapy because they will provide real evidence of your worth. They will counteract any crippling doubts that you may have. After all doubt, like any other feeling, is only a product of your imagination.

An expert, one who can truly boast a long list of achievements, is worth a lot of money in the market. Sometimes an awful lot. Not because they demand a high salary, but because they are in demand.

5.3
Keep your finger on the pulse

Information, like money, makes the world go round. So be attentive to what is happening around you at all times.

Start by listening and observing within your immediate professional circle. What are the department's problems, projects and challenges? Is the management considering taking on more staff or restructuring? Listen to the rumour mill, too, without forgetting that whatever you hear might be true but it might also be totally false. Chatting with people over lunch or at the coffee machine will teach you a great deal. Don't hesitate to take your coffee break on another floor so you can chat with staff from other departments. Then you can sort and filter all the various pieces of data you have collected on the subject that interests you.

Take a quick look through any reports available to you, and check the internet for news concerning your company and its business sector. Read the press releases published by your company directors. Seek out the profiles of newly appointed directors. Are they specialists in business development or cost-cutting? Peruse business-to-business publications, and consult the websites of rival firms and read their annual reports. Look at their strategies, their annual results and the profiles of the people they are hiring. Compare their strategies to those of your company and develop your own opinion.

By gathering information in the simple ways mentioned above, you will be able to detect not only opportunities for success but also potential threats to your survival.

Sometimes you might discover that the various data you have collected are pointing to a major crisis and the imminent demise of your company, so be ready to jump ship before it sinks. All ships can sink, regardless of their size, so keep a good lookout for potential hazards looming on the horizon. Even if you are good at what you do and your projects are profitable (even very profitable), the thousands or millions of dollars that you have brought into the company will never be enough if the company's losses are in the order of billions.

Whatever you do, you need to generate value. If your company's prospects for survival are good and the current crisis is merely a passing storm, you will be one of the many hands contributing actively to keeping her afloat. Your endeavours and contributions will probably get you noticed. If the company's prospects are dire and you feel that the situation is hopeless, your efforts will allow you to tread water during the first wave of redundancies, and give you a competitive and interesting profile to hawk around the job market. Whatever happens, be good at the duties you were hired to perform and committed to the success of the projects you undertake.

Having a strategy is fundamental to your success. Diligently executing your daily tasks and guiding your value-generating projects to fruition is the course you should set for yourself. Information will help you deal with obstacles in your path, to anticipate them, avoid them and even confront them. The successes you achieve as you go about your normal duties and the special projects you undertake in parallel will provide you with the necessary skills to deal with difficult situations and bounce back when things go wrong.

Are you good at what you do and recognized as such? Are you an investment which generates more than it costs, and can you prove it with reliable figures? If that is the case, then you are well equipped for any situation that might come your way. If, in addition, you are well informed and able to anticipate the situations to come, you have will become a formidable player in the workplace.

5.4
Work on your weak points

A weak point is a potential danger and could prevent you from bringing your projects to a successful conclusion. It is therefore imperative for you to identify your weaknesses as objectively and as honestly as you can.

Sometimes it is very difficult to identify your weak points. For any given weakness you might, for example, decide to simply ignore its existence, only have an inkling of its nature, or just not have the right words to express it. You might also be scared of facing the truth and so you minimize or disregard a particular weakness. Society often exerts considerable pressure, and in a world which values superlative performance above all, admitting to weaknesses – however natural they might be – can engender a deep feeling of anxiety which results in their denial.

If you need help, ask a trustworthy friend to tell you what aspects of your personality, behaviour or professional expertise they think you should improve. Obviously you shouldn't take their opinion at face value, but it is worth listening to. It is up to you to be selective and forge your own opinion.

Focus on the weaknesses that could hold you back or prevent you from achieving your objectives, and then sort them into an order of importance. Which ones are critical and which ones are minor?

In general, weaknesses can be organized into two broad categories: psychological and technical.

Technical weaknesses are legion and involve an insufficient knowledge of, for example, a particular computer application, a foreign language, sales skills, communication techniques, or the current legislation governing your field. You can only rectify technical weaknesses by learning, by educating yourself. Fortunately there are very inexpensive solutions to be found on the internet and in books. Study those skills which are necessary for your survival and your success, in particular ones that you can expect to use regularly in the future. If you are thinking about learning a language, understand that you will need to go through several years of intensive training. Ask yourself whether you will still need this language by the time you have acquired it. And if so, for how long? Learning a language that you won't need is a total waste of time, unless of course it is your hobby and you like exploring new cultures.

Psychological weaknesses often involve a limited group of emotions. Foremost of these is fear. That paralysing fear that prevents you from moving out of your comfort zone, that prevents you from running a risk, pressing ahead and taking the initiative. There are lots of solutions for overcoming psychological weaknesses, but you will find that they tend to disappear once you start racking up the successes. The hardest part is getting the virtuous circle started. Books and training courses – by people who have actually achieved something – are worthwhile solutions. I have always found the biographies of politicians and business leaders to be very inspiring. The philosophy of the Stoics has been useful too. If you know a good psychologist or a good life coach, that might be an option for you but watch out for charlatans as they far outnumber the true professionals.

Remember my experience with a fantastic personal trainer who helped me regain my self-confidence? Sport has helped me solve professional problems regardless of the fact that the two aren't, in my case, really connected.

A final point: developing skills and reducing weaknesses both take time and you should consider them an investment. So carefully target your weaknesses and identify the fastest, most cost-effective way of turning them into strengths. Invest your time and effort into gaining knowledge that is worth your while. Forget the rest.

5.5
Develop time-saving tools, automate basic tasks and focus on high-value projects

Time, as the saying goes, is money. And we have already looked at the importance of making time.

If like many jobs yours involves a certain number of simple and perhaps repetitive tasks which could be automated using a spreadsheet program such as Microsoft Excel, then automate them! Create your own tools and routines to save precious time that could be put to better use, such as acquiring knowledge, managing high-value projects or simply taking the time to relax.

If you are responsible for a team, take the opportunity to delegate routine work and any low-value tasks to your subordinates. Concentrate on high-value tasks and educate yourself to ensure their success.

The more you work on complex projects and tasks that generate high value, the more you put a lid on attacks from your rivals, make your position secure, and increase your value in the job market.

5.6
Offload any activity that doesn't generate high added value

As mentioned earlier in this book, you should target activities that generate high returns and do your best to offload unrewarding tasks that have little or no added value.

In addition to developing tools to process work that lends itself to automation, you can also delegate. You could say that automating tasks using a spreadsheet program like Microsoft Excel is, in fact, delegating work to a computer or an algorithm.

If you can't delegate it, transfer it. When your normal duties and your cost-optimization project are taking up a lot of time and, on top of that, your boss comes to you with a routine and very basic task, suggest allocating it to the latest addition to the department's workforce or to an assistant. After all, it would be a shame to delay the implementation of your cost-cutting project...

Negotiate your workload and avoid wearing yourself out with too much overtime. A real professional is someone who sells his expertise via a contract. When you dine out at a restaurant, the chef will cook what you have ordered. Sometimes he or she might offer you coffee, a drink or perhaps the dessert on the house, but they will never spend two extra hours in his kitchen just for you, and never for free. That seems pretty obvious, and yet how many executives work overtime every day? Over a single week, two extra hours every evening is equal to spending one long day in the office. Over a year, that amounts to working fifty-two extra days – long ones, too – for free. That's huge.

Yeah, but it makes a good impression because you are working hard and are devoted to your company, right? Stop playing the martyr! First of all, nobody is taken in by such pious behaviour. Also, you will see just how much your devotion weighs in the balance of the next redundancy scheme. Be professional.

Lawyers, doctors, tax specialists, consultants, technical experts and the like all invoice their customers for the time spent on the job because they are professionals. By not accepting and applying this principle, you are admitting that you are not good at what you do and, as a result, compensate for a lack of quality by increasing the quantity. What's more, your colleagues will view you as a pack donkey that they can keep on loading on the cheap.

Be professional. Estimate the workload that is compatible with the time indicated on your employment contract and make sure you reflect that when you set your annual objectives. If a superior wants to give you an additional task, negotiate the terms. Which of your less important duties would your superior like to assign elsewhere to free up time for you to undertake this new task? It isn't possible? Well fair's fair, accept to do this new task in exchange for a raise.

Induce opportunities. Why don't you suggest a minor reorganization of your duties so that you can concentrate more on projects that have the potential to generate added value? Your manager could think about it and, if they agree, allocate a certain number of your less important tasks to other colleagues who are less inclined to protest.

A real professional creates added value. You will never become a real professional by accumulating tasks that create little or no added value. So you should offload them. All these unimportant tasks are heavy weights that prevent your career from taking off.

5.7 Set aside more time for you

The donkey that wears itself out putting in long hours every day and working weekends is rarely very productive. Don't count on it if you have to run a marathon, and even less if you need to win a sprint.

If you want to be good at what you do, you must carefully manage your efforts and your fatigue. On any normal day, your first hours at work are the most productive. As the day progresses your endeavours become less and less efficient. Economics students will be familiar with this problem as the "law of diminishing returns".

We often talk about how our professional life and our private life are separate, but in truth you only have one life whose time is divided between work, rest and play. Yes, only one life. So you really need to find a balance between these three aspects of your life. A satisfying personal life will improve your chances of having a successful and rewarding career. A job that you can do well without exhausting yourself will improve your chances of enjoying health, happiness and fulfilling relationships. Satisfied people achieve more and are better at convincing others because they radiate positive energy and it feels good to follow them.

Working hard for nothing doesn't make any sense. Working intelligently does. Working hard and intelligently is good, but only for a cause you hold dear, and for a well-founded life goal.

Be a professional. Perform your duties and fulfil your contract of employment. Negotiate raises and promotions based on your results and nothing else. Do not allocate your time carelessly because it is your life you are giving away for free. Unless of course you consider your life to be of no value. Do not ask for charity but instead sell the investment that is you.

Do not be scared to rest and relax. It is necessary. Doing nothing or watching a light-hearted film can do you a lot of good. Laughter is important. Humour is a formidable weapon when faced with adversity. Don't be scared of solitude, of taking time to be on your own. Your spouse will certainly need time too, and you don't have to be together every hour of every day in order to have a meaningful and loving relationship.

Your time is an asset that belongs to you. Invest it wisely. The more you have, the more you can invest in endeavours you consider worthwhile and useful. A day lost to fruitless overtime hours could have been invested in a couple of hours learning something new, three hours on value-added projects, and the remainder on rest and leisure pursuits.

The value of your time can be easily calculated by dividing your income by the number of hours you work. You know how much your time costs per hour. The further you progress, the more this value increases. If you do the ironing yourself, and your hourly rate is $130, then you are losing money. Hire somebody to iron your clothes for you and use the time for yourself.

Don't forget to set aside time for the ones you love. Instead of enduring pointless hours in the office performing duties that will not help you grow, spend time with your family, with those you love, and honour their affection for you by sharing your precious time with them.

You don't have time for them? Be prepared to deeply regret it one day.

6
Take Risks, Calculated Risks

Risk-taking is often considered to be a dangerous act, fraught with peril, and one to be avoided. I'm sure people have convinced you not to do something on numerous occasions, saying something to the effect of "You're taking a big risk!" Well, avoiding risk is the best way to never do anything in your life.

People who discourage you with such words are usually the kind of person who puts their savings in the bank (and gets fleeced by their fees), forms relationships which are devoid of love or any kind of shared project, gives advice on love without ever having experienced it, gives advice on how to manage your career without ever having had any real success in their own...

People like this never take risks and, consequently, make the worst decisions. They work for their bank and not for themselves, make themselves unhappy in love, and drag their spouse into a downward spiral of boredom and regret. Risk avoiders never make progress in their career and content themselves with feeble wage rises and titles which often mean very little other than to flatter their petty ego.

And yet, everything we do every day involves some sort of risk. Every time you cross the road you are taking the risk of being run over by a car. And what do you do? You check both ways and then cross. If a vehicle is heading in your direction, you estimate its distance and its speed, and then decide whether you have enough time to cross or not. In other words you take a risk but, without really thinking about it, you take a certain number of precautionary measures to ensure that your crossing is successful and doesn't provoke an accident. You take a calculated risk. And you take dozens, perhaps even hundreds of calculated risks every day without even thinking about it.

So if you want to get to the other side of the road, you are going to have to take risk, a calculated risk. Surviving and progressing in the workplace are just the same. If you want to get promoted, you are going to have to take risks, calculated risks. The task might be more complex than crossing the road, but the principle is the same. You have probably forgotten the first time you had to cross the road and how hard it was for you as a child. Today it is a piece of cake. Being shorter made the task more difficult because you couldn't see over the vehicles, and of course you had never done it before. Today when you cross the road you apply the various safety measures without even registering that you are doing it. It has become a reflex. It is the same thing for your career.

In this chapter we shall look at some of the risks and opportunities I have experienced in my career. Just like when I crossed the road for the first time, I was initially scared of taking risks in the workplace. But if I hadn't done so, I would probably still be occupying a minor position, attracting little interest and commanding an insignificant salary. It was worth every rush of excitement and stress I experienced.

6.1
Choose your projects, pick your targets

Regardless of whether you are managing numerous projects full time or just a few in addition to your everyday duties, you must ensure they are all successful. Many projects fail because either they were very poorly selected or the associated risks were poorly assessed.

Foremost, do not take on projects that are unrealistic or too ambitious. Unless you are the director of a major group with hundreds, perhaps thousands of people at your disposal, you will likely undertake your project on your own or with the help of a small team. With such limited means you won't be changing the face of the company. If you are working alone or with a couple of colleagues, and have a lead time of a year, you must target your action very carefully. A pilot study is ideal in these conditions. Limit the scope of your project to a manageable size, and pull out all the stops. In this way you will increase considerably your chances of success and if the project doesn't work out, its limited scope will ensure that your failure goes unnoticed in the eyes of your colleagues. In the case of a successful outcome, you will be able to gradually extend the scope of your endeavour to ensure your development in the company over a period of several years. Start small, and expand.

Next, make sure that you are getting involved in a project that has real added value, one that can generate extra savings or turnover for the company. Updating a data sheet is pointless if it does not lead to increased sales or save money or time. Instead, all you are doing is wasting the company's time and money. Not to mention that you strip yourself of all credibility by showing your colleagues that you have nothing better to do than devote yourself to useless tasks.

Assess carefully your strengths and weaknesses in relation to the project. Set aside time to undertake this essential preliminary task. Simulate in your mind how the project will unfold. What will you need exactly? How will you get it? When will you get it? Who or what has the potential to hinder the project at any given stage? How can you deal with or avoid these hindrances? In short, carefully think (and think again) about how you are going to carry out your project before you set the wheels in motion.

Do not ignore obstacles that you are likely to come up against, such as resistance to change, tense relations between individuals or departments, enthusiastic supporters who, once the project gets going, leave you in the lurch... Integrate uncertainties, what the Prussian military theorist Carl von Clausewitz called "frictions", into your plan. Managing a project is nothing like operating precision machinery. Managing a project involves pursuing an objective along a path littered with pitfalls and unexpected events.

Never underestimate the risk of someone hijacking your project. Some colleagues are past masters at appropriating other people's work. Others are expert in the art of observing projects and joining them once there is no longer any risk for themselves, most of the hard work has been done and success is just around the corner. Your immediate superior could be in this category.

So when you choose a project, bear in mind all the abovementioned considerations and keep an eye open for other similar pitfalls. Assess your strengths and weaknesses, and the risks and opportunities of each project that you are interested in pursuing.

During this selection process try not to be put off by real or potential obstacles. Do not think in terms of whether you can or cannot undertake a project, but rather how you are going to undertake it. Do not think in terms of whether you should or shouldn't take on a project because of its inherent risks, but rather how you are going to overcome or avoid its risks. If you don't, you will likely saddle yourself with a mindset that paralyses you, forcing you to remain static and thus vulnerable to attack. Approach your projects like a predator its prey. You can see the opportunity in the distance, it is up to you to figure out how to reach it.

6.2
Legitimize your projects and make that legitimacy known

Nothing is more dangerous than undertaking a project for which, on the face of it, you have no legitimate role. It is a gamble which might make your fortune or just as easily ruin you.

So don't gamble, at least not in an amateurish way. Take meticulously calculated risks and only meticulously calculated risks.

If your role within the company authorizes you to undertake projects as a matter of course, then your situation is relatively simple. If you are allowed to undertake cross-departmental projects, that is to say projects which involve departments outside your own, then it is desirable that you obtain the approval of those department heads before launching the project. In all cases, make sure that you have at the very least the prior approval of the management.

If your role doesn't normally allow you to undertake these kinds of projects, you will need to adopt another strategy. As mentioned earlier in this book, you will need to secure the support of your senior manager and then your immediate superior.

If your project has the support of your hierarchy, that is to say at least your immediate superior and your senior manager, any risk of your project being hijacked is considerably reduced because you have a mandate to take action and can request cooperation within the company. Equally, it will be harder for someone to put a spanner in the workings of your project. If somebody does try, then he or she will be obstructing your hierarchy, perhaps even the top management, which is rarely a good idea.

If your job is more focused on executing rather than implementing and managing projects, then you will have to legitimize your request to undertake a project. Your superiors might well feel a bit jittery about letting you embark on a particular adventure when you haven't already proved your worth in that area and the outcome is far from certain. You will have to reassure and convince your hierarchy.

First of all, your work must be irreproachable. If your work is meticulous and reliable, then your management will have developed a certain amount of confidence in you.

Next, your analysis of the situation must be robust, the rewards must be tangible and the actions must be simple and realistic. In addition to having confidence in you, your superiors will then have confidence in your project.

You will now have to manage the objections. "What have we got to lose?" they ask. "Nothing," you reply. Take responsibility. It won't affect the performance of your normal duties. You can organize milestones to explain in total transparency the successes and problems you have encountered, and the simple solutions you intend to deploy to overcome the obstacles. Managers are rarely entrepreneurs and tend to have a visceral aversion to risk. By behaving in this way, you will reassure them and encourage them to invest in you the legitimacy you need to manage your projects.

When your role involves almost exclusively the execution of tasks, you need to move slowly. Do not commit more than 10% of your time to developing projects. This allows you to start out safely. It is better to learn to shoot in a shooting range rather than in the middle of a battlefield... Next, your manager won't be concerned that your official duties are going to suffer, which is a priority. Lastly, by undertaking projects in a limited capacity, your immediate superior will not feel particularly threatened by any success you might have. Once your initial projects have been achieved successfully, gradually increase the time you spend on projects during your working day, and don't forget to show this in your annual objectives. After a few years of success, you can quite easily be in a position where you are spending 50% of your time on projects. However don't exceed this percentage.

After a while you should start considering opportunities for promotion, whether in-house or in another company.

Legitimacy accumulates gradually over time, and in proportion to your successes.

6.3
Make yourself known to the executive management

It is only in the eyes of others, in particular those of your management, that your status as a professional can ever be established. Think of the fake, self-proclaimed experts who have been parked in some dead-end part of the company and contribute no value. Superficial types like them never go very far.

Being recognized by senior management as a professional who contributes real added value to the company is the ultimate accolade. When the executives consider you to be an investment for the company, that is the first sign your career (and your salary) is getting off the ground.

If your role in the company doesn't naturally bring you into contact with the executive committee, do you best to get as close as possible to its members.

Apply the previous examples given in this book, such as project pitches in the elevator or in front of the coffee machine. Try to learn more about the difficulties currently being experienced by the company and in particular those where you can contribute to improving the situation. If certain difficulties directly involve your department, it is an excellent opportunity for you to offer your services...

If certain top managers are involved in the same after-hours activities as you, that's also a great occasion for getting close to them. Belonging to a club (sports, art, music, wine-tasting, etc.), volunteering for a charity, canvassing for a political party, or any other hobby or interest are all promising opportunities for sharing experiences and creating bonds. But you have to be true to yourself, don't fake it. Don't join the cigar appreciation society if you don't like smoking. Don't join the same football club as a senior executive if you don't know how to play football. Losing a match because of your two left feet is unlikely to endear you to him and won't serve your interests at all. Only take part in activities that you like and enjoy doing. Never do an activity just for the sake of furthering your career because your self-interest will soon be exposed.

Try to take part in meetings where senior managers will be present, so your face becomes a familiar one. Once in a while ask a question to gain an insight into, for example, the potential consequences or causes of a particular problem that you could turn into an opportunity for developing a project. When you suspect a point on the agenda might harbour a potential project you could use as a vehicle to demonstrate your worth, look carefully at the subject and if it turns out that an opportunity does indeed exist, propose during the meeting to look into it further. You can prepare a costed assessment before the meeting to expose the extent of the problem and justify the need to take action, and then you can volunteer to explore the issue.

Get noticed when acknowledging the contributions of those who helped you on a given project by copying in their most senior manager, unless of course the distance between you is too great to be credible. When you are working for, say, the Spanish subsidiary of a large German bank, you could copy members of local management into your thank-you emails. However it would almost certainly be bad form to include the group's CEO in Frankfurt. It is up to you to find the right balance.

Human resources management is also a good bet if you don't have direct access to the executive management. Too often people tend to reduce the function of the HR department to hiring, paying and firing, whereas an equally important task of the department is to keep talented personnel from leaving the company. Also, armed with your results from the preceding years, you can firmly justify and negotiate your request for a rise or a promotion, or both. If your arguments are well founded, human resources will register them and submit them to management for review and approval. Consequently, the top layer of the company will get the opportunity to discover your name and what you have achieved.

Getting noticed by senior management is essential and there are many ways you can do this. Neglecting this fact can result in wasted time and missed opportunities because, unless he or she is also on the executive board, your immediate superior is unlikely to have the power (or the desire) to give your career a boost.

6.4
Managing relations with your immediate superior

Relations with your immediate superior might be cordial and uncomplicated, at least on the surface. They might also be downright execrable.

Never forget that you are working in a competitive environment and not a collaborative one, despite the official communications extolling the virtues of team work. If the players in a team really did adhere to the collaborative spirit, then there would be no need for a captain.

Bear in mind the various objectives managers might have (we looked at this earlier in the book) and certain fundamental principles.

Principle number one: your immediate superior is your boss. They are not your friend. Nor are they a guru to be followed blindly. They might be good or bad in terms of what they know and how they behave. You can admire them or detest them. Whatever the case, they are your boss and when the day comes for them to choose between their head on the block or yours, their decision will not be the result of a long and profound reflection, but instead the fruit of a simple reflex to survive. Additionally, I have noticed that when there is a conflict between an employee and their immediate superior, the management tends to side with the immediate superior.

The risk in this instance is allowing your relations with your immediate superior to deteriorate to the point that they actively affect your ambitions and become your enemy. Your survival is at stake, as are your chances of success.

First of all, give them respect. Being on the receiving end of an official warning for not showing respect does not bode well for your survival, and even less for your success. If relations are good, so much the better. If they aren't, force yourself to say

"Hello", "Goodbye", "Please" and "Thank you", and hold the door or the elevator out of courtesy.

Next, you should deliver the work expected of you. This work should be meticulous, reliable and beyond reproach. You must not leave yourself open to attack because of the quality of your work. Work the hours expected of you, without going overboard. Make sure your annual objectives are compatible with the working hours set in your employment contract, otherwise you might find that your goals are unrealistic and you cannot fulfil them, which in turn makes you vulnerable and unable to set aside time for projects or yourself. Whether relations are good or bad with your immediate superior, these simple principles are essential. Your performance must be based on tangible and objective facts, not personal feelings, tastes or opinions. In doing this, you will show your immediate superior that you have no intention of hindering their own goals. It is an approach which will serve all parties well.

Guide your projects to fruition. They will contribute to your success and make your position in the company secure, as well as trigger new opportunities for success. Your immediate superior will benefit from your successes by association.

Support your immediate superior when they need help. If you sense they are in difficulty, in a bad position, offer them your hand and do your best to pull them to safety. If they are having a bad time in a meeting, help them get through it. If somebody attacks them about a particular piece of business, you can always interject that huge efforts were deployed but there just simply wasn't enough time for the finishing touches. Request an extension to the deadline so you can finalize the job and integrate all the pertinent suggestions made during the meeting. Of course, if the situation is dangerous and your support for your immediate superior might actually make you vulnerable, then keep your distance so you don't get dragged down with them. Lastly, if your immediate superior has got it in for you, there is absolutely no reason for you to offer them a helping hand, especially if it gives them an extra chance to hasten your downfall.

Every manager has a different personality. As a result, it is impossible to generalize but you should always be prudent. Bear in mind that the peaceful and sunny beaches of the Caribbean are also the theatre of cataclysmic cyclones every year.

Be prepared for your relations to deteriorate and even become conflictual. It isn't always going to happen, of course, but it is nevertheless a risk worth considering. If everything goes well, your efforts to avoid this risk will have contributed to your inner peace. On the other hand if the situation gets out of hand, your efforts and prudence will be well rewarded.

First off, don't be entirely dependent on your immediate superior. Make yourself known to your senior manager, even their own manager, and develop good relations. Arrange it so that they are aware of what you are working on and the associated issues. By doing that, you will prevent your immediate superior from appropriating your achievements, even if they do it surreptitiously.

Also maintain close links with human resources management. Even if the HR director is out of your reach, you can still maintain contact with the person who is responsible for your career within the company. Tell them about what you are working on, your current projects, the associated losses or missed earnings, and the gains you aim to achieve.

And in general, make sure that a maximum number of people are aware of what you are working on, your current projects, the associated losses or missed earnings, and the gains you aim to achieve. Also, broadcast your achievements and the amounts they have made or saved throughout the company. Don't be ashamed to repeat yourself, I know I do! It will contribute to your reputation and make it harder for a malicious manager to carry out their underhand intentions.

Don't join a clan. A company is sometimes divided into rival camps. There is always a winner and a loser. And a new arrival always has the potential to turn today's winner into tomorrow's loser. Even if your relations with your immediate superior are tense, do not throw yourself into the welcoming arms of an opposing clan. Stay on good terms with all the clans and don't take sides. Keep your focus on the tangible results of a job well done. That doesn't mean you can't occasionally talk with certain colleagues about the difficulties you are encountering and, whenever possible, how much the tensions with your immediate superior are costing the company...

Time is sometimes an excellent ally. That immediate superior who has been causing you problems might announce that they are resigning or moving to another post. Suddenly your problems might resolve themselves without you lifting a finger. I say "might" because you don't know anything about his or her successor, who could be just as malicious and perhaps even worse.

If your immediate superior's behaviour keeps getting worse, if they cling to their post like a limpet to a rock and nothing seems to be able to knock them off their perch, if your situation appears hopeless and you are suffering, then you should start thinking about looking elsewhere. If you like the company you are working for, keep your ears and eyes open for in-house opportunities. If not, monitor (discreetly) the job market, use your network to put out feelers, and start to apply for positions in other companies.

For my part, I have had numerous bosses. Some competent, others incompetent; some frank, others devious; some brave, others cowardly; and so on. I have had to deal with all sorts of characters. In about half of the cases, everything went well, some very well and I encountered no problems. In about 30% of cases the situation could be considered "normal", in other words neither good nor bad. In about a fifth of the cases, the situation was tense and I really did suffer.

Once again, it is impossible to generalize because each situation is made unique by the people involved, their stories and the context. I am only sharing the lessons I have drawn from my own personal experience. Suffering at work because of the actions of a hostile superior is an all-too-common occurrence. Talks to resolve the situation often fail because the actual causes of the problems are often too subtle and too difficult for the malicious protagonist to admit.

There is no point in making negative assumptions when the relations with your immediate superior are good. Just be prudent and never forget that he or she is your boss.

6.5
Take up a new post, change company

During the twentieth century it was very common for an employee to spend his or her entire career in the same company, but those days are long gone. You will probably take up a new post several times in your professional life, perhaps because you lost your job or an opportunity to progress presented itself and you seized it with both hands.

Unless of course your reason for moving was redundancy, taking up a new position involves various risks that you should think carefully about.

The first risk of changing voluntarily your job is the very real fear of not being up to the tasks required of you. Will the management ask you to exploit certain skills and experiences you don't have? Are you really worth a higher salary? Do you really want to change department or company and leave behind a comfortable situation, a familiar workplace and colleagues who have become friends? Will it be too difficult? Is it really the job for you? Indeed, thinking along these lines will make sure you flunk this new post because you are completely demotivated and probably won't even send off the application. You will spend more time looking for excuses for your inaction and regretting your indecision rather than actually applying for this attractive new job. This quote from Richard Branson springs to mind: "If somebody offers you an amazing opportunity but you are not sure you can do it, say yes – then learn how to do it later!" In my experience he is absolutely right. I have never possessed more than 80% of the qualities and skills needed to perform the new post I managed to secure. Sometimes I had 100% of the competencies required for a job that I didn't get. Does that job offer look good to you? Do you want to advance your career? Well, go for it! Seize the opportunity. You might have an uncomfortable six months, followed by a slightly more comfortable six months, but in the end you will be operating in your new environment like a fish swims in water. You will have taken a giant step. You will have progressed in your career, probably secured a higher salary, acquired new skills, experienced new situations and, above all, you will have overcome your fear.

The second risk involves leaving a company where you are at home. At least, that's how you feel. You are leaving a known environment for an unknown one. Often you will be terminating an employment contract which seems to you stable in order to undertake a trial period which is by definition uncertain. You might fear (once again) that you won't be up to the job and the trial period will end in disaster. I have rarely seen someone fail to complete their trial period successfully. On the other hand, I have seen hundreds of employees lose the job that they believed to be theirs forever, and they didn't see a thing coming. Statistically it is more likely you will be made redundant rather than fail to complete your trial period.

The third risk is leaving to join a company that is not very stable, perhaps even a speculative venture which might at any moment take off or go bankrupt. You'll be like a hungry little mouse looking at a tasty piece of cheese sitting on a trap. Go hunting for information beforehand and look closely at the company's history, its sector, its reputation, reviews of its products and services, its turnover over several years, its profitability, and any links it might have to a larger entity that might intervene if the going gets rough (which might also be an opportunity for you to advance your career). By doing this you will be able to make your decision based on factual information. You will find it easier to answer the question: Do I put in my application or not? What you should never do is let your emotions rush your decision.

A fourth risk involves the nostalgia you might feel for your previous job. You might miss the good old times. It might have been better before. That's all well and good but you are in the here and now, working for your current employer. Keep your comparisons to yourself and look steadfastly towards the future. If you don't, there is a danger that somebody might wonder why you ever changed company and then suggest you should have stayed there. If you acquired knowledge and skills in your previous work experience that could be put to good use to improve the situation in your new company, keep them to yourself for a while. Observe the situation over several months, and prove your worth to the company. Once you are established, use these hidden assets to develop projects which will raise your profile in the company.

As a general rule you should always look seriously at any opportunity to advance your career, regardless of whether you have to change company or department. Some opportunities only come along once. Estimate your chances of success and if you have doubts, remember what Richard Branson said.

6.6
Moving abroad

Have you ever thought about looking further afield to boost your career?

The first time I took up an international post was not out of choice. It was imposed by events, in particular the fact that I couldn't find a suitable job at home so I started to look across borders to other countries. The fear of change tied my stomach in knots, not least because I still didn't speak the local language properly after years of lessons. I found it difficult to change. Living in a new city, speaking a new language and discovering a new culture, alone, surrounded by strangers, was a major challenge. If you have already experienced expatriation, you will know what I am talking about.

However I have never regretted making a choice that boosted my career enormously, adding sparkle to my life and allowing me to live several lives in one.

Once again, the risk you face is being paralysed by the fear of taking action. As far as I'm concerned these events were what pushed me to leave, otherwise I would have probably never moved away and never discovered what I had been missing. If I no longer fear moving from one country to the next, it is because I have done it before and now know that, even if it is a difficult thing to do, it is worth it. Almost all the expats I know are in the same situation and wouldn't hesitate to up sticks and move abroad if the game appeared to be worth candle.

Nevertheless there are some preliminary considerations to be taken into account.

First of all, you need to be ready to make the leap. By "you" I mean you and your family if you aren't single. Would your family be willing to follow you to a new country where they might have to speak a different language and might have to adapt to a very different culture to the one they are accustomed to? Is your family willing to move away from the grandparents? If your spouse has a good job, would they be willing to give it up? What kind of life can your spouse expect to lead in this new country? The opportunity to boost your career might also be the cause of your marriage's demise if you don't consider the consequences of a move very carefully.

Once you have established that your family is willing to follow you, the adventure can begin.

Make sure you have signed a contract with a major local or international group, unless of course you are intending to set up a business yourself. Local companies are often willing to pay handsomely in order to attract new talent, so don't limit your search to companies from your home country which have an international presence. In addition to good pay, which might also come with many other advantages, such as your employer covering your accommodation, comprehensive healthcare and your taxes, you will often get the chance to occupy a post that would normally have been out of reach in your native country. That latter point is fundamental. Your employer will generally help you with all the cross-border paperwork and setting up home, either directly or via a company specializing in such services.

The benefits are usually enormous. Nevertheless stay alert for certain risks which could compromise your integration.

You are going to a country which is not your own, one that has its very own culture, rules and perhaps language. Consider yourself to be a guest and behave in accordance with the local rules. Rather than criticize them, try to understand how they came about. Your will learn a lot, especially about yourself. Read up on the local culture before leaving and once arrived, ask the locals for advice on how to act in any given situation that might be an issue. They will be delighted to help you. While you might not feel it necessary to become fluent in the local language, do at least learn some words and phrases if only to demonstrate your respect for their culture and your intention to integrate. Some subjects might be taboo, such as politics and religion, so don't bring them up. Nevertheless, do try to understand where the differences come from. You will probably be surprised to discover some of your ideas and convictions are false.

Make sure you know about the country you are going to. Some countries are politically unstable, some close to civil war, and you risk placing you and your family in danger. It is preferable to choose politically stable countries and be ready to get out at the first sign of danger.

Respect local laws and get advice on them before you leave. You can consult guidebooks and websites, in particular those published by embassies. What might seem normal to you is in fact prohibited in some countries. Enjoying a tipple from your favourite bottle of Scotch whisky might get you into serious trouble in some places. Likewise, possessing a few grams of hashish might get you a heavy fine, a few months in prison or, in some countries, the death penalty.

Over time you will start to feel as though your roots are loosening their hold on you. Out of sight, out of mind, as the saying goes. The distance between you and your native country will gradually increase until contact with home will be restricted to your loved ones. After a time living in the local culture you will probably start to adopt some of its characteristics. If you meet your future spouse in your new country, the collision of cultures will almost certainly produce some agreeable surprises, as well as some tensions that only patience (and plenty of it) can overcome.

Moving abroad is, in my view and in the view of other expats I know, an excellent opportunity. Not only do you get a unique chance to propel your career and your salary to new heights, you will also enjoy the benefits of living another life, perhaps starting over again. Many expatriates decide never to return permanently to their former life, to their former home country. And that's not without good reason.

Living several lives in one, especially in pleasant and comfortable conditions, is a chance not to be missed. In my opinion, obviously.

6.7
Setting up your own business

Who hasn't dreamed of being their own boss? The idea has probably crossed your mind as indeed it has for most of us. This option could be your path to success and happiness, but you might encounter some very difficult moments. Yet another risk that has to be thoroughly calculated before taking any action.

For a start, don't rush into setting up your business based on a whim or a feeling. Setting up your own business necessitates thorough preparations and solid foundations. I have seen many former colleagues, both engineers and financiers, react to turbulence in their career by deciding to jack it all in and open a restaurant. None succeeded and most of them lost everything. They might have been good at cooking for six people, but cooking for fifty at the same time is another kettle of fish. A professional cook spends several years at school, not unreasonably, to learn the trade. In addition to the cooking, they also have to manage the suppliers, the accounts, the advertising, the health and safety issues, the staff... All that just to turn a profit.

Regardless of the type of business you want to set up, whether a restaurant or a consultancy, you need to be sure of your capacity to carry it off successfully. It isn't just about your motivation, but also the motivation of your potential customers to seek you out and pay you properly. You need to have a demand that you can supply, preferably a sustainable one. So watch out for sudden changes in the economic situation, progress in technology, new techniques, and unexpected trends and fashions. You will also need sufficient capital to finance the launch and see you through the first six months to two years in business. Thereafter, your working capital needs to be enough to cover at least three months' business so that you can absorb any unexpected expenses and, more generally, just continue to operate.

More and more salaried employees, in particular executives of a certain rank, become consultants for their former employer. This can be an interesting option if it means you get paid better or enjoy more free time. It can be even more interesting if you can count on several clients to launch your business and provide you with lucrative contracts for the first few years.

On the other hand, being self-employed means that you have to take responsibility for all the administrative costs and taxes. In some countries you will be required to pay social charges right from the start, even when you haven't generated the slightest turnover. If you are a sole trader, your business will stop running whenever you are ill or on holiday. You will probably have to do more work than before not only because of the administrative load previously borne by your employer, but also because your customers will become even more demanding in terms of standards and deadlines. If you have several customers, your workload might become too heavy to handle.

When a company enters a cost-cutting phase, the first to have to tighten their belts are the consultants. Then come the temporary workers and finally the salaried employees. So when times are hard, you will be among the first of those to be impacted. You are also vulnerable when your contact in the customer's company moves to another post. Your new contact might want to continue collaborating with you, even to increase your business. But he or she can also decide to reduce or terminate your collaboration, for objective reasons or on a whim.

Having an idea, a project, an ambition and a dream are all essential to the human condition and we all yearn for independence. It is just that we need to reassure ourselves that our actions will be enough to realize our dreams so they do not become nightmares. Do you want to be self-employed? Well, look into it thoroughly first. Prepare a solid business plan for your project, including all the worst-case scenarios, an analysis of your strengths and weaknesses, and a list of all the risks and opportunities. Think about how you are going to mitigate those risks and develop those opportunities.

Once you have completed your preparations, acquired the knowledge and analysed the situation you will be in a much better position to make a decision. To do this job, you will need to be able to set in motion all the points mentioned previously in this book: a dream, a goal, a mindset, solid skills, a liking for a job well done, time (plenty of it), a real capacity for listening and observing in order to identify potential opportunities and threats, good health and the support of your family and friends.

7
Communicate, Communicate, Communicate

I often hear people say that communications and marketing are a waste of time. If that were true, then why is advertising seemingly ubiquitous in every aspect of our daily lives? Why do politicians spend so much money on election campaigns? Why do companies spend so much money on marketing? And why do we communicate with each other so much?

The simple answer is that communicating competently is beneficial. We all like to dream and we all aspire to a better, more comfortable life. Politicians who run a good campaign get elected. A good advertising campaign can boost the sales of even the most insignificant of products. How can a bottle of flavoured water full of sugar, hinting at some magical experience other than the more probable weight gain, sell for such a high price? Because advertising works.

Consider too the effectiveness of word of mouth. It is the best publicity of all because it is viral. Consider also the many inanities that almost all of us swallow in one way or another because they have simply been repeated over and over again until they become a belief or "truth" in our insufficiently enlightened minds.

If you are to succeed, and not just survive, you cannot allow yourself to ignore a promotional tool as powerful as advertising. After all, if you are so good at what you do and your projects have created so much added value for the company but nobody knows about it, what is the point?

You are a product on a market. You are an investment on a market. Other people should know. You should make sure they know, continuously.

7.1
Demonstrate your efficiency in meetings

Meetings are an important arena for advertising. You should behave professionally. Your contributions should be based on facts, concrete actions, verifiable results, and simple explanations.

The less you speak, the more your contributions will get noticed. If you speak in order to convey accurate observations and simple, realistic solutions, your words will be heeded. If you are recognized within the company for your professionalism, not only will your words be heeded, your opinions will also carry weight in decision-making.

Those who speak all the time, monopolize discussions, propose costly projects based on vague observations or theories and never produce anything but waffle, end up being ignored. Sometimes they even become the company joke, the clowns whose uselessness becomes ever more apparent with each successive utterance.

Listen. Take notes. Try to understand other points of view. Identify points of contention and what generates them. Explore and propose solutions that attract a consensus, so that everybody wins – with you in pole position.

Limit your contributions to a few minutes and get straight to the point. If you have to make a report, retain only the three most important points backed up with reliable figures. If you have to propose an action, quickly remind the meeting of your report, backed up with figures, and reiterate the issues your action will target and the results it is expected achieve. Offer your services. Be eloquent, efficient and demonstrate that you are someone who takes action.

As previously explained in this book, meetings are an excellent source of opportunities. Learn how to seize them. Only participate in meetings where you can be of use or identify opportunities. Don't waste your time attending a meeting just to show your face, unless of course you are obliged to take part. You have got better things to do. It is also better for your image if you don't get tarred with the brush reserved for the pointless-meeting chumps.

7.2
Make yourself known to your superiors

This bears repeating once again: your superiors should be aware of you and you should be in contact with them. You obviously know your immediate superior, but what about his superior? And the person above him? They should know who you are, what you have achieved and what you can do in the future. Ideally, the management should know who you are.

Your contributions in meetings, your achievements and your visibility in the company will help you achieve this, but it will take time and require diplomacy.

If you are unable to make yourself known directly to your hierarchy, there is always the human resources department. Your performance appraisal interview, your results and your requests for promotion and better pay are all systematically forwarded to your superiors for approval and, as such, will make you known to them, albeit indirectly. And their interest in you will only grow if your appraisals are positive and your added value is carefully measured and accrued year in year out.

7.3
Make yourself known to all your colleagues and managers

When you want to water a plant, you can either shower it from above or rely on the raising properties of capillarity. It is exactly the same when you want to raise your profile within a company. Best of all, promote yourself from the top down and the bottom up.

Previously in this book we looked at how you can maintain connections, develop your network and obtain information about what is going on in your company by asking discreet questions at the coffee machine, during lunch or over drinks after work. You can also use these situations to communicate on your achievements, backed up with a few figures. Advertise your achievements without resorting to excessive boasting.

The news will soon get round the company. And it will be added to all the feedback issuing from colleagues you have worked with, managers you have met or informed during thank-you sessions, meetings you have contributed to... Your reputation will only benefit and grow.

7.4
Make yourself known outside the company

Despite your efforts, it might be that your company can't or won't promote you or worse, might decide to dispense with your services altogether. It might be that you consider your future to be in another company, perhaps even in another sector. While advertised job vacancies can be a rich source of opportunities, it is very often word of mouth and personal recommendations that produce the best results.

Service providers, suppliers and other partners working with your company also work with many other companies, some of which are rivals, others not. Imagine for a moment that you are a financial director looking for someone to supervise the accounts department. After discarding all the potential candidates already working in your company, you will probably ask an outside accountancy firm or people in your wider network to suggest a suitable candidate.

If you work with outside contractors, you should maintain good relations with them. A working lunch, drinks in the evening: seize all the opportunities for getting to know them better, and for promoting your skills, knowledge and achievements. In a word, make yourself known outside your company and in the sector you are targeting.

The added value resulting from your projects will be a real advantage that will make the difference, especially if you have generated for your company more money than it pays you. You will become a prized and therefore expensive asset in the job market.

7.5 Learn how to use a presentation program

Good verbal and written communication is essential. Good verbal, written and graphic communication is an asset. And good graphic communication requires mastering the use of a presentation program such as Microsoft PowerPoint.

It is the best kind of tool for making presentations in front of executive committees, wherever in the world they may be. This book is not the place for a lesson on how to make a slide show, but it is worth mentioning a few key points that are often overlooked and make your presentations, and thus their message, less effective.

Firstly, your presentation should tell a simple story founded entirely on facts. Try not to exceed ten slides because if you do, you risk losing the attention of your audience. Stick to a simple format, for example a costed analysis of the problem or opportunity, its causes, the solution (including costs and benefits) targeting the aforementioned causes, risks associated with the solution and their prevention, and the action plan.

Next, do not include too many details that clutter your slides and make them illegible. You can go into the details verbally during your presentation, focusing on the key points. If someone wants to hear specific details on a particular point, you should be able to give the answers without hesitation. Giving a summary presentation doesn't mean you have a summary understanding of your proposal. On the contrary, you should have comprehensive knowledge of your subject, right down to the smallest details.

Make your presentation look good. If your company doesn't have a standard template, make your own. It should be of a sober design that doesn't smother the contents but ensures they stand out. Take a tip from the adverts produced by Apple: white background, a photo of the product, and a key message backed up with a few important details. Simple, carefully made slides rarely disappoint.

Avoid including anything that might anger a member of the audience, otherwise be prepared to make an enemy. Speak of "results not being as good as hoped" rather than "poor results", "a lack of suitable resources" rather than "incompetent colleagues" and so on. Softening your message makes it less dangerous.

When presenting your slides in public, make sure you never read the text on display but contribute content that isn't visible. If, for example, you are presenting a map of the world which displays increasing sales figures, do not read out the figures but instead point out the countries which are experiencing strong growth thanks to increased volumes, those enjoying growth which can be attributed to favourable exchange rates, others that have had their results boosted by the launch of a new product, and so on. Be concise and don't forget your goals are to convince your audience of the opportunity and to get approval for your action plan. Present this action plan in the form of a table which describes the various phases, a preliminary schedule and, most importantly, an approved/rejected column to encourage the management to make a decision on each proposed action.

For my own presentations I tend to limit myself to five or six slides and a maximum of fifteen minutes, which leaves plenty of time for answering questions and discussing actions. The latter can never be approved in their initial form. So set aside time at the end of the presentation to make the necessary changes with input from the room, in particular the decision makers. Once they have taken part in drafting the actions, it will be hard for them to disapprove of the project later. And your little manoeuvre will have done the trick!

7.6
Master the art of rhetoric

If you are a lawyer, a politician, a philosopher or an art critic, you will know that rhetoric (the art of persuasive speaking) is a very powerful tool. It can convince people to adopt foolish ideas and reject worthwhile projects.

This is made possible by the fact that the vast majority of folk listen to their emotions rather than reason when making decisions. Used with benevolent intentions, rhetoric can help you optimize your presentations, your speeches and more generally all your contributions to society. It is also a useful weapon against those who might use it for malicious purposes, in particular against you or your company. I encourage you to read the excellent book The Art of Being Right by the German philosopher Arthur Schopenhauer, often quoted in numerous works and videos on the subject.

Some prestigious schools and universities organize eloquence contests which can be very instructive to watch. They also organize exercises where, after having defended a point of view, the student must then defend the opposite point of view. The results can be astonishing.

Be prepared for numerous underhand tricks. For a start, someone can turn your arguments against you or use a simple counter example that is sufficient to discredit your proposal. Your legitimacy and your expertise can be cast into doubt. Someone can pull the rug from under your feet by diverting the debate to a subject that is more favourable to them. You can also be put off by an avalanche of questions not always related to the subject in hand. An opponent might force you to go into all the details to demonstrate that your project is too complex and too ambitious to be debated in a general meeting, or even to be implemented at all. Your words can be twisted. Your convictions and your beliefs can be used against you. Sentences or phrases can be quoted out of context to make it seem like you said the opposite to what you were actually proposing, which is something of a speciality for certain journalists. Doubts can be cast over various points in your proposal in order to demolish it entirely. One of your arguments can be pushed to the extreme or exaggerated until it appears utterly ridiculous. In short, there are lots of ways to get you flustered.

Your achievements and results are the best weapons to use against these kinds of attacks. The greater your credibility and prestige within the company, the more the management will support you, and the more resistant you will be to malicious rhetoric.

Add the art of rhetoric to your personal training programme so you can anticipate attacks and be equipped to fend them off. It will hone your capacity for effective communication and optimize your negotiating skills.

7.7
I and We

Unless you are giving a very personal opinion, systematically use "we" instead of "I" in your presentations. It changes everything.

It is reassuring to hear "we". A decision maker will be more comfortable allocating a project to a group of people rather than a lone individual, unless of course he or she has known you for years and considers you their right-hand man. Betting on several horses rather than one increases your chances of getting a payout at the end of the race. It is a natural reflex to want to spread risk. So if your project involves a team, be sure to say "we". If you are running the project on your own, be sure to mention that you will be collaborating with several departments.

And the "we" will follow you. Your collaborators will feel more involved in your project if you say "we". In fact you break down the barriers erected by the use of "I" and "you". By using "we", you will make them feel as if they have a stake in your report, even if they might question certain aspects of it. They will feel implicated in the actions you are proposing.

Using "we" initiates a sense of solidarity. The words "solidarity" and "solidity" share the same etymological root, and by using the solidarity of "we", you will add solid foundations to your reports and your actions. Involving the group will encourage the group's involvement. In the case of success, it will be a collective win. In the case of failure, the responsibility will not fall on a single individual but on a collection of individuals, thus diluting the risk for each person involved and making the decisions easier. The group dilutes the sense of vulnerability. The group facilitates collaboration and thus your project's chances of success.

By replacing "I" with "we", your communication will be more powerful, more effective and more convincing. You won't just be a creator of ideas but a real player in the team and a (potential) leader motivated by the success of each and everyone involved.

8
Dangers to Be Avoided and Confronted

Throughout this book we have looked at risks that could hinder, even thwart your progress and success. So let's review some of the most dangerous.

8.1
Your immediate superior

The subject of the immediate superior has come up multiple times.

During your career you will almost certainly have to work under a succession of managers. And dealing with each new manager is like playing roulette, sometimes even Russian roulette. You might have five good bosses in a row and then number six wants to get rid of you for reasons that might be entirely objective or on the other hand, difficult to admit out loud. Never forget that we are all human. Our instincts and emotions often override our reasoning. A boss who doesn't like you because, for example, you risk casting a shadow over him or her, your car is better than theirs or you aren't the type to say "Yes" to everything, is a boss who will give you a hard time. Your career can be brutally hobbled by a hostile manager who crosses your path. You might even find yourself in the unemployment aisles if they manage to get their way and boot you out of the company.

Your best weapons to prevent this are respect (at least superficially), a job well done, communication with your senior manager (your boss's boss) and good relations throughout the company. Never allow yourself to get boxed in by your immediate superior because you could find yourself in an uncomfortable position. Everything can run smoothly over many years until the day when it is every employee for him or herself.

Alternatively, you might never have the slightest problem with any of your immediate superiors, and I hope that turns out to be the case. We are after all dealing with risks and not certainties.

8.2
Diversification

As with everything, diversification is good if practised in moderation. It can be harmful when taken to excess.

Your time and energy are limited resources. You can't satisfactorily manage ten projects all at the same time. You need to reduce your ambitions in the short term, which doesn't mean you have to reduce them in the long term. Sort your ten projects by order of importance and every year select two or three that you can put all your efforts into. This will increase your chances of success and, thanks to a schedule filled with viable projects, render your position secure for the next three or four years.

In addition, your stamina will increase. You won't wear yourself out so easily, you will have time to relax, to learn, to be with the ones you love, to develop new projects, and to explore new interests. You will avoid getting burned out, unlike those who take on too many tasks in order to shine brighter than their colleagues. There is nothing wrong with wanting to light up the company firmament, just aim to be an enduring star rather than a flash of lightning.

Diversifying your activities in a measured way is good. It is better to have two or three projects on the go, knowing that one might fail, be abandoned or suffer delays. Similarly it is always a good idea, for prudence's sake, to have several sources of income and spread your investments across several types of assets.

8.3 Tiredness

Tiredness is a major danger. When you are tired, you are no longer productive. It is time for a break to recharge your batteries.

First, make sure you prepare for tiredness. Manage your time, maximize the amount of free time you have, and factor in rest, moments on your own and periods of silence. Ensure you get quality sleep. Exercise, even if it is just a daily walk. Take care over what you eat but don't forget to enjoy yourself either.

Once you feel tired, don't try to fight it. Forget about downing ten cups of coffee a day or guzzling energy drinks. Certainly you will eke out some extra time before the crash, but you also risk suffering a harsh longer-term reaction. It is pointless trying to fight tiredness, just take a break. A long weekend can reboot your energy after a sluggish period, and two or three weeks' holiday can be enough to wash away more serious fatigue. Enjoy a change of scene, a trip to the seaside or a hike in the mountains. For my part, a week on the Atlantic coast is enough to bring my energy levels back up to normal. Keep an eye on your emails, just in case an emergency or a serious setback crops up while you are out of the office. Do not reply to any non-essential emails. Just enjoy your holidays in the knowledge that you can clear your inbox when you get back, not before.

Tiredness is a formidable enemy. It affects your judgement, pushes you into making mistakes, makes you bad-tempered, and damages your relationships. Working systematically through tiredness is more likely to lead to your burning out rather than achieving success.

Most successful people structure their day so they can optimize their energy and avoid tiredness. A lifestyle founded on quality sleep, well-organized working days and time set aside for rest and leisure pursuits will surely contribute to your success.

8.4
Broken Promises

Breaking a promise can result in you losing all credibility, regardless of the merits of the excuse you put forward to justify yourself. Professionals who don't stand by what they say are simply full of hot air. They are superficial, hollow, and don't even respect themselves.

It is absolutely essential that you manage the expectations of your collaborators. Only promise what you are certain to be able to deliver. If you can't be sure that a given project will be completed by a particular date, you can always promise your colleague that you will do your utmost to meet the deadline, while insisting on the fact that you are in no position to offer guarantees. Choose transparency and honesty over ambiguity and weasel words. In the long run it will pay dividends.

Real professionals are motivated by results. Their commitments must be as reliable as the quality of their work. Real professionals are credible.

8.5
Yourself

Contrary to what you might think, your immediate superior isn't the greatest danger to your survival and your success in the workplace. Neither is it tiredness nor spreading yourself too thin. No, the biggest danger is... you!

Survival and success are the fruit of a constant struggle against yourself.

First, you have to combat your inner demons such as fear, desire and jealousy. Fear can hinder and paralyse you, prevent you from taking action. Desire is positive when it helps you determine the goals you want to achieve. But it can also be a source of frustration and resentment when, instead of setting goals for the purpose of better achieving them, you focus on dreams and then imagine all sorts of reasons that prevent you from realizing them. Your failures will be caused by the rich, by politicians, by a virus... in short, by anything other than yourself. Jealousy will make you toxic, even to yourself. Unlike kindness, which will efficiently help you progress, jealousy will isolate you and push you to take malicious actions and say nasty things. Does your neighbour have the type of car you would like for yourself? Well, think about how you could buy yourself one rather than heap imprecations on the poor man.

Next up are addictions, which are very dangerous. Alcohol and drugs are the first addictions to spring to anybody's mind, and they can indeed be very dangerous. However you can get addicted to many other things that can hinder your steady progress, such as food, sex, fame, power, video games, TV series, and social media. As with anything, excess is dangerous, but as long as it is legal, it doesn't mean that you have to deprive yourself entirely. Addictions prevent you from maintaining an absolute control over yourself and eat up lots of your time, money, and energy: in short, the three things you need to survive and succeed in the workplace.

Lastly, your education, your beliefs and your convictions can also turn out to be dangerous. Many of us do things automatically, without really thinking about them. When confronted with the question "Why?" we answer with something like "That's how it is", "It's how we do things" or "It's a tradition". Many people just parrot back information that they have heard or read without actually thinking about what they say. Some assertions can even be imposed by the mindless majority and anyone who tries to uphold a different opinion, regardless of its merit, is immediately ostracized from their society. In this instance, learning is the key. Acquire knowledge continuously. Learn about the technical aspects of your business, and about science, philosophy, history, psychology, art... Compare points of view, including the least popular ones, try to understand where they come from, and develop your own opinion. Understanding how things are done is important. Understanding why things are done is even more important.

Parents often teach their children principles that they believe to be good. And some are good. But others can hinder progress. How can you achieve success if you believe that wealth is disgusting, that ambition is reprehensible, that trying to make dreams come true is for idiots, or that taking risks (even calculated ones) is pure folly? The truth is you need to be able to identify what is good for you and what is harmful. Just because everybody does or views something in a certain way, doesn't make it fair or true. If it were, then the Earth would be flat and travelling at speeds greater than 30 mph would kill you. Hmm, that's a good example of rhetoric, too!

In addition to inner demons, addictions and various harmful teachings and convictions, the other huge danger to be avoided is not loving yourself. Nothing forces you to love you as you are, and nothing forces you to remain as you are. Retain and maintain your strong points, the ones you love. Develop and modify those traits of your personality that bother you. Are you too fat? Take care of yourself and re-energize your body through regular exercise and a better diet. If necessary, get help from a professional. Is your job a drag and you feel like you are stagnating?

Take action! What do you want to do? Set yourself goals and establish a plan for achieving them. Are you addicted to TV series? Set aside a specific time in the week for watching your favourite show, or treat yourself to the box set as a reward when you complete a project successfully. Does your hair look a mess? Make an appointment with the hairdresser. Do you find yourself ugly? Treat yourself to a session with a beauty specialist, you might be astonished by the result. In short, there are always plenty of solutions on offer, especially in the internet age.

Your little demons are in you and are part of you. Let them express themselves but don't let them dominate you.

8.6
Integrity

In the workplace, the golden rule is this: do your job and undertake your projects with integrity. Never break this rule.

It might be tempting to use your position to obtain certain favours, to supplement your income, or to doctor certain figures in order to obtain a bonus or a promotion. Well, watch out, because it could all go horribly wrong. You would certainly be reprimanded, perhaps given an official warning. But you could also lose your job, get sued or even worse. Your life could be turned into a living nightmare for a price that wasn't worth paying.

Always be transparent with your figures, your sources, and your sums. Be sure to conserve all your work files and sources documents, preferably on a server. When using spreadsheets, exploit wherever possible the formulas that allow you to follow the path from the source data to the final result. Do not hide any doubts that may hang over a particular figure and instead of presenting a single amount, show a range extending from the worst to the best-case scenarios. Do not embellish your results in order to stimulate your annual bonus or to force a decision. Some of your colleagues might doctor their figures, perhaps with a certain artistry, but keep them at arm's length and don't be tempted to do the same.

Never lie to your management and never omit data that could have an influence on their decisions.

Condemn all types of harassment, whether psychological or physical. If you want to get rid of a colleague who is incompetent, causes serious problems or behaves inappropriately, do not harass them but instead stick to the facts and remain objective and courteous throughout the dismissal process. Are you dreaming about a workplace romance with a colleague? If they refuse your advances, harassing them won't change their mind and behaving in that way will certainly expose you to serious disciplinary measures. If on the other hand they accept to enter into a relationship with you, think about the possibility of your falling out in the future and the consequences it could have on your professional relations. And what happens to your relationship if you have to discipline your lover who is also your subordinate? These consequences are worth considering before giving free rein to your amorous feelings. If you don't, you risk losing out both professionally and personally. Make sure your relationship doesn't generate conflict in the workplace. Choose someone in another department or with whom your professional dealings are of little importance.

Steer clear of all sorts of favouritism and any behaviour that might give an advantage to somebody at the expense of others. Frustration and hostility are powerful enemies and should not be created lightly.

Avoid all forms of corruption, under-the-table deals and brown envelopes. Otherwise you will get caught up in a dangerous spiral of lies which risks destroying your career, your spirit and even your family. You will end up living in the permanent fear of getting caught. It is a dangerous game, as unpredictable and desperate as Russian roulette.

Your reputation is a crucial asset. It takes years to build, but can be demolished in an instant. Maintain and improve it with tangible results that are obtained through honest and ethical conduct.

8.7
Keep a close watch over your colleagues

Don't trust anybody in the workplace. Keep your eyes open. Keep an ear to the ground.

Listen out for rumours, especially those that involve you. Rumours can be the source of many an opportunity, but they can also be particularly malicious and do you a disservice. You need to put an end to them rapidly, extinguish them with the facts. If, for example, a rumour is doing the rounds which accuses you of doctoring your figures, at every opportunity use concrete examples to show your colleagues how your figures are calculated. Show how your sources are researched and corroborated, how your sums add up, how your data is freely available on the company's server and – most importantly – how your work is 100% ready for auditing by anyone at any time. Facts should be sufficient to extinguish any rumour.

Some rumours can be more serious. If rumours of your supposed corruption or fraud are circulating, show zero tolerance and demand an investigation by the internal auditing department or the human resources department.

Is the word going around that you are going to be assigned to a dead-end job? Make an appointment with your senior manager to see if the rumour is indeed true and, if so, to find out why. You might well find that they are even more surprised about the news than you. Do the same if you hear about your imminent dismissal or the promotion of another colleague to a position for which you are objectively better qualified.

The only way to keep up to date on the rumours circulating around the workplace is to have a good in-house network. Often your prattling colleague will open with "I shouldn't be telling you this but..." and close with "I'm counting on you to keep this to yourself because I wasn't supposed to tell you." Your network will be all the more efficient if it comprises a lot of connections, if people have good memories of working with you and if you are well regarded by your colleagues.

Sharing secrets is a double-edged sword, however kind the intention of the sharer, because your own secrets risk being broadcast around the workplace. Sometimes it just takes a little forgetfulness on the part of the person with whom you shared your thoughts, and your secret is well on the way to becoming common knowledge. So be very prudent and as a general rule, soak up discreetly shared secrets like a sponge water, keep other people's secrets safe (which will strengthen your reputation for reliability), and do not share your own secrets with anybody (at all).

Don't forget that every piece of information needs to be double-checked and its source verified. The same goes for rumours, too.

9
Towards Independence

As you are reading this, you might think I often repeat myself. Well, that is true because I do. But it is also deliberate. Repetition is the cornerstone of learning.

And I will say it again: the contents of this book are only a selection of the lessons I have drawn from my personal experience in the workplace. They are in no way an exhaustive inventory. This book could never be a universal manual for survival and success in the workplace, and certainly not a miracle recipe. What works for me might not work for you, and the opposite is true too.

I managed to protect my position in the workplace, to progress and to significantly increase my salary over the course of just a few years. My current position is relatively good and the risk of me ending up in the unemployment aisles is pretty remote (unlike my situation fifteen years ago). Yet the risk isn't completely at zero, especially in the long term, and for as long as I am a salaried employee, the risk will always be there. A new boss might not appreciate me. A major and very costly mistake might be impossible to forgive. The potential causes of my future dismissal are many and varied.

If there is one fundamental thing that I have understood, it is that you need to develop several income streams and not rely solely on your salary, regardless of the successes under your belt and the position you occupy in the hierarchy. If I lost my job, what would I live on?

Inadequate state and private pensions, accidental injuries, unexpected expenses and the many other factors that can impact income have to be taken into account, which is why prudent professionals diversify their revenue streams and do not rely solely on their salary or retirement payments.

In this book I have shared with you how I managed to make my job more secure, more sustainable and more profitable. The resulting savings in time and money have allowed me to undertake new activities, such as writing, while I continue to develop my financial independence.

With each passing month my peace of mind increases. My career could stop at any moment and I wouldn't find myself in any particular difficulty, and certainly not in the situation I was in several years ago.

My skills and my achievements are well known in my business sector, and in a certain number of countries. In terms of productivity, I have managed to position myself among the top one percent of my profession. Several of the largest companies on the Fortune 500 list have offered to take me on if my current employer was no longer satisfied with me or I with it.

The time I managed to free up has allowed me to develop a personal investment project and devote my time to writing, which gives me an occupation.

You should see yourself as an investment and invest in yourself. And every investor worth their salt invests in various assets. Do not invest solely in your salaried work.

Here follow some ideas and food for thought.

9.1
Work less, earn more

Optimizing your time so you have more of it is one of the keys to success. Wasting your time doing unpaid overtime is a nonsense. Working two extra hours per day will diminish your hourly rate. Certain executives who work a huge amount of overtime sometimes find that they are being paid less per hour than a cashier in a supermarket. If that is the case, why not be a cashier? Two hours' overtime per day amounts to ten hours per week or forty hours per month, and over eleven months, it is equal to 440 hours or in other words twenty-seven days a year. Yes, two hours' overtime amounts to working for free for an entire month every year! Not only that, you are selling yourself cheaply and losing as much credibility as you are money. True professionals never do that. High-level consultants, lawyers, doctors and head chefs will all charge you a fair price for doing extra work. And if they give you something for free, don't worry, they know they can make up for it later.

Is your boss exploiting you unfairly and eating up all of your free time? First things first, assess the situation. How much do you cost your boss? Next, how much do you bring in to the company? Bosses rarely exploit good investments unfairly. On the contrary they tend to pamper them, so long as they don't push their luck too far. And if they do push too far, their luck might just drop off a cliff.

If you bring in profits of $500,000 a year and your boss refuses to pay you more than the minimum wage, change your boss. Compare your situation to advertisements for similar positions in your sector. How much does the market say you are worth? If you are more profitable than most of your counterparts in the same business, then place yourself in the upper echelons of the wage range. That way you can carry out your very own annual assessment by comparing your salary, your achievements (duly costed) and the salaries being paid in the sector. If your company can't or won't do anything, say nothing and discreetly look for a new position that pays better.

With more free time on your hands, not only can you educate yourself, rest and relax, and spend more time with your loved ones, you can also develop complementary activities. Some of these activities will further your progress along the road to financial freedom. If you have the time, the possibility to save money and the right state of mind, you have all the cards you need for a winning hand in the game of success.

9.2 Develop your intellectual freedom and objectivity

Independence isn't just a question of money. It is also a question of intellect.

Human beings tend to follow the crowd, fall in with every fashion, subscribe to the commonly held opinion and even adopt the verbal tics of prominent people. This isn't a defect of behaviour. It is just deeply ingrained in our nature. We are made like this. However, sometimes the crowd runs headlong towards catastrophe. Stock market crashes are an excellent example of this. Masses of individual investors, often inexperienced in the world of finance and guided only by their emotions, their greed and their fear of missing a unique opportunity, rush to put their money into the latest thing, creating a bloated market bubble which, when it bursts, causes financial ruin and many a personal drama.

This is why you should never adopt the opinions of the masses and never repeat parrot-like the assertions of a stock-market hack, even one working for a renowned media outlet, without first making your own opinion. Compare different points of view, even those that the majority consider extreme or eccentric. Explore all the various arguments and take a close look at their foundations. Are they based on figures, on historical facts or on populist sound bites that aren't worthy of your attention? Read up on the subject, analyse and study the sources, understand how the figures were produced and on what basis, identify the origins of the problem... Analyse trends, historical data and cycles over the long term. The Web contains a mass of data which you can easily compare and corroborate.

This mindset has allowed me to implement innovative strategies in my line of business and to achieve professional success when only a few years ago nobody would have thought it possible. Everybody was adhering to the opinions expounded by so-called experts and the assertions of newspaper articles which quoted those selfsame experts. All I did was study the history of my business sector and the price of raw materials since its inception, something that clearly none of these so-called experts had done. Several books and a few statistics gathered on the Web allowed me to understand issues that the recognized experts could not (and still don't), and enabled me to generate several hundreds of millions of dollars of added value while the experts failed to make even a single cent.

9.3 Become an expert consultant or a teacher

If you are good in your field, you can monetize your expertise as a consultant. In addition to the extra money, you will also gain in visibility and experience.

You can raise your profile by creating a website, taking part in conferences, writing and publishing articles, or hosting a YouTube channel. On the other hand, you can just rely on your network of contacts or existing opportunities. It is up to you. Setting up your own enterprise will teach you lots of new and often fascinating knowledge, such as the administrative aspects of founding a business, accounting and taxation, communication and marketing.

You will also need to set aside enough time for this new activity, which might turn out to be a failure, a success, or even the first tentative steps of a new life. Be ready to lose the capital you stake in the business. If it is a success, that's great. If you hit the jackpot, even better. If you fail, you will have lost your stake but you will have also gained a unique experience and new competencies which will serve you for the rest of your life – and very likely for a future project. You will have lost your capital investment but you will have gained a superb personal investment.

Before moving ahead with your business project, make sure your consultancy activities won't conflict with your salaried position. As a general rule, avoid working for companies who have direct or indirect dealings with your own. If you are in doubt, read through your employment contract again, consult your human resources department or a lawyer to make sure your business initiative won't compromise your salaried position. Also call on the services of an accountant to help you not only with your bookkeeping, but also with the creation of your business and with taxation issues. Last but not least, don't devalue yourself by providing services under the going rate.

You could also start teaching, if your experience and qualifications are suited to the task. You could either teach as a professor, if you have the right diplomas, or as an outside contractor. In both cases, you will have to be willing to take on an additional and probably poorly paid workload for preparing your lessons and marking your students' work. Except for the top tier of the teaching world, most people earn no more than a modest living from education. That said, it is still a great way to get yourself known and could be a springboard for starting a consultancy or writing reference books for students and professionals who wish to self-educate.

9.4
Turn your salary into assets

This isn't necessarily the best option, but it is the one I prefer.

My lifestyle is relatively simple and by increasing considerably my salary, I have also significantly augmented my capacity for saving money every month. What's more, by keeping my lifestyle simple – although comfortable – and not falling into the trap of acquiring luxury accessories, I have been able to optimize my capacity for saving money.

Some use their savings to buy consumer goods or repay a mortgage for the house or a loan for the car of their dreams. They purchase liabilities and get poorer. Others invest in assets, that is to say goods and stocks which create wealth by accruing value or by naturally generating additional income, or both. They acquire assets and get richer.

Investing in assets, in particular financial ones, requires you to have a sound understanding of what you are doing. You don't need a master's degree in finance, but you do need to acquire real financial knowledge which can only be learnt from those who have achieved success and who know how to make the most out of an investment. Without learning the ropes first, you will increase considerably the risk of making poor investment choices, and you will also run the risk of seeing your profits (severely) diminished by the often-enormous commissions deducted by banks, investment funds and other intermediaries.

Not only that, financial consultants are often just salesmen who promote the financial products that pay them the highest commission. There is no guarantee that the products that pay intermediaries the highest commissions will actually generate the highest profits for you. Many investment funds make handsome profits. However, once you have paid the various commissions (management fees, intermediation costs, custodial fees, and so on), social charges and taxes, there's not much left over for you.

Research has shown that the performance of reputable investment funds rarely exceeds, over time, the performance of the financial indexes. Commissions deducted by index funds, such as exchange-traded funds (ETF), are generally lower than those practised by the banks and other traditional investment funds, so investors will find them very competitive. The possibility of purchasing and selling index funds through online brokers at reduced rates makes them even more competitive and, as a result, they will increase your potential profits by allowing you to make considerable savings on management fees and commissions.

Diversification is an important principle to which you need to adhere. Certain rules should be followed and modified according to your appetite for risk-taking. Diversification can apply to the geographical zone, the type of asset, the business sector, the maximum percentage per line in your portfolio, the type of counter-party and more. You need to weigh up all these considerations before investing your money.

Compound interest is also a marvellous friend to have. One dollar at ten percent a year, a level of performance that certain indexes can easily achieve when the economic situation is good, can rise to $2.50 over ten years, $6.70 in twenty years and $17.40 over thirty years. If you can invest $100, $500, $1000 or more a month, do the sums. As your career progresses in the workplace, your salary increases, your capacity for saving increases, and your prospects for making a fortune increase. You will realize that financial independence is within your grasp. The further you advance along this route, the less fear you will have of being unemployed or having to live off a meagre pension. Instead, you will become more independent and more self-confident.

Any time you manage to free up can be used for your self-education, and throughout this book I have insisted on the necessity of freeing up time for oneself. Without suitable training, investing in assets is a dangerous enterprise. I highly recommend that you first invest in your financial knowledge and once acquired, then and only then do you start investing in financial assets. You will learn, for example, that ETFs aren't generally a financial basket that mirrors an index, but a fund that replicates an index. It is very difficult to resell thousands of shares in stocks used, for example, for the international indexes and certain "tricks" are implemented by the ETFs, although not without some risk. You will need to learn about certain markets, such as the precious metals market in, notably, gold and silver. And of course you will have to understand your fiscal obligations so that your profits don't get swallowed by income taxes that you could have legally avoided. In short, it is not something you enter into lightly and you really need to undergo a real and in-depth education in the subject.

Never forget the effort you made, the time you invested and the difficulties you had to overcome in order to build up your savings. The less you know, the more likely you risk losing all the money you managed to set aside. The less you know, the more likely you risk losing everything.

9.5
Develop a personal project based on an idea or an interest

When I look at media platforms like YouTube, I am always astonished by the number of videos made by enthusiasts of all kinds. Cars, history, animals, model-making, cooking, gardening, watchmaking, wine, painting, sculpting, stamp collecting... The list is long. After making a few videos, many entrepreneurs have gone on to develop channels which attract absolutely enormous numbers of views and provide their authors with an extra revenue stream. If you have an interest you are passionate about, why not embark on an adventure of this kind? You would certainly enjoy exploring your interest, you would discover a new medium for communication and you might even earn a bit of money.

Do you think you are not very talented when it comes to making videos? Just take a look at the successful YouTube channels. The videos are usually very well made. But then look at the very first videos posted on the channel and you will probably see that the quality wasn't quite as good. That's normal. As with everything, there is always a period of learning.

You could go into teaching, volunteer for a charity, invest your time in a cause you hold dear. In most cases you won't be making any money, or very little, but you will feel that you are making a useful contribution and making people's lives better. Being active in a different professional setting, even without getting paid, would certainly provide you with an immense sense of satisfaction.

You could write books, create works of art, cook, do consultancy work, draw comic books, help out with DIY, design interiors or exteriors, develop software, set up a sports club, invent board games... The possibilities are endless.

By freeing up time and increasing your capacity for saving, and as a result the amount of capital you can bring to the table, you will be giving yourself the opportunity to take on projects such as the ones I mentioned above.

And what if it doesn't work? Once again my answer is the same: You will lose the capital investment, certainly, but you will gain considerable pleasure just by having a go. You will learn a lot and feel more confident, too. And nothing prevents you from drawing lessons from your mistakes and giving the adventure another go later.

Whatever the outcome, the main thing is you will enjoy yourself. If it makes money, so much the better. But whatever the result, you won't be one of those people who, at the end of their life, regret not having given it a go.

As I write this book, I say to myself that if it helps just one person to keep their job, to get a raise, to feel better about him or herself and to feel happier, then I will have achieved my goal. I will have been useful even if, when the dust settles, it will have cost me time and money. And if the time and money I invest ends up generating a profit, so much the better.

9.6 Trading

Trading is a fascinating subject.

If you want to get rich, trading is certainly an appealing proposition. It is just a click away. The dream life, easy and comfortable, is within your grasp. It can transform a life of hard labour into one of enchanting leisure. And all the hoards of self-proclaimed experts (I'm being polite) who claim that trading is an easy route to wealth and requires little more than a few hours' work, and all the Hollywood films depicting the get-rich-quick schemes of Wall Street traders contribute to keeping the myth alive.

If there really is a master stroke that can make your fortune, it only works for an infinitesimal minority of traders, regardless of whether they are professionals or amateurs. And for most amateurs, the profits are modest and the losses frequent and often ruinous.

Trading isn't just a hobby, despite its popular image. You can't just read a couple of books, watch a dozen videos on the internet, buy a trading station, open an account with an online broker, and then expect to be successful in an instant. No. It is an art which requires a lot of training before you start. Professional traders generally come from the very best business and engineering schools on the planet, and that is not a coincidence. And let me dispel another myth: most traders don't earn millions in bonuses every year. Once again, only a very small minority achieve such wealth.

The first step on the road to being a successful trader is education, learning the business just as you did for your day job. You can start by watching a few videos online, but you will soon have to read a vast array of books and probably undergo some formal training. Whether it be videos, books or formal education, you should choose content that has been produced by recognized professionals who have had real experience in trading at major stockbroking firms or banks.

And your training will take time, especially if your initial education wasn't in finance. Not only will you need to learn about trading but you will also have to understand the fundamentals of economics, be able to determine whether a company's stock price is accurate, too high or undervalued, and be familiar with the basics of risk management. You will need to gain some legal skills in order to understand the framework of the markets, as well as the risks that you will expose yourself to when you sign the contract with the stock broker or bank.

And you will also have to learn about psychology, in particular crowd psychology and the psychology of investing, and more generally about behavioural finance. You should understand the mechanisms leading to markets overheating. These are often characterized as irrational blips but the truth is they always have a rational explanation. You should learn to control your emotions. Controlling your emotions when stock prices are fluctuating, when you have to deal with an avalanche of contradictory data, when you are facing risks, and when you have to understand the group effect, in particular relating to social trading. You should learn how to resist being influenced by the often very convincing speeches of get-rich-quick salesmen selling "once in a lifetime" opportunities. You should learn how to resist your own thoughts, your feelings of loneliness, your frustration in times of trading inactivity, your excitement when opportunities arise, your pride when you make a profit and your despair when losses occur. Your mental preparation will be a determining factor in your success. You need to have nerves of steel.

You will probably focus on a particular type of trading. Scalping, swing trading, trading the news... The options are numerous and all require specific expertise. Next, what type of products do you want to trade: FOREX, shares, options with or without leverage, gold, silver, crypto assets, oil, agricultural raw materials, indexes...? Once again, you need to think carefully before deciding. It is essential that you know exactly what you want to trade before you start developing your strategy.

You will need to learn the fundamentals of risk management. First of all you need to optimize the structure of your portfolio in order to render it less risky without comprising on the performance goals you have set. Fixing limits on positions, analysing correlations between assets and the many other fundamental points are not to be taken lightly. You will also need to fix yourself rules for buying and selling, and think about using stop-loss orders. Various tools like this can assist you in managing risk, but that doesn't exempt you from having to learn and master the fundamentals.

While investment is a very different kettle of fish from trading, bearing in mind its basic rules will help you keep your feet on the ground. Are you ready to speculate on the stock of a company which has been losing money for five years, which offers no prospects for turning a profit, and whose share price continues nevertheless to rise? How much are you willing to lay out for this stock? How much are you ready to lose?

You will also have to decide with whom you are willing to work. A bank or a broker? If you are going to buy a structured product, which fund do you choose? While the cost of the commissions is an essential and determining criterion in your decision-making, don't forget to read the contract in its entirety. Not many people do. And many regret it – usually once it is too late.

And once again, remember that trading isn't a game. The market is by its very nature uncertain. Trying to predict its course is a challenge. The judicious course of action is often just to accept the uncertainty of it, in other words, the fact that anything might happen, rather than try to predict what might occur. You will be competing with a multitude of traders, both amateur and professional. You will also be competing with a multitude of hardened professionals who are assisted by experienced analysts and systems that can react in a nanosecond. You will carry very little weight compared to them, and even less compared to a market that operates without the slightest emotion.

If you are interested in trading, then have a go, but only after much reflection and suitable training. Don't enter into it nonchalantly or like a fruit-machine player in a casino. Trading, like investment or any other business, is a professional activity which involves taking or avoiding enormous risks. Be careful not to add your name to the long list of amateur traders who lost the stake they were prepared to bring to the table (and sometimes much, much more).

9.7
Real estate

Real estate, just like trading, isn't an adventure you want to embark on lightly. Successful property investments require preparation, knowledge and expertise.

Real estate can be a good way to build up your investment portfolio and a significant source of income thanks to its potential for leverage. The risks are also numerous. Investing in a rundown property in the wrong locality, renting to an unreliable tenant, getting clobbered by taxes or a difficult economic situation are just some of the many factors you need to take into account in your business plan before entering into the real estate market. If you don't, the fruit of your hard work over the years might well just be gobbled up for no gain, or worse.

Once you have a significant sum of money to invest and the capacity to purchase a property, where do you start looking? First of all, focus on areas where you can resell the property if need be, for example an area where demand is naturally high (a sought-after district, good schools, good public transport, dynamic local economy, reasonable taxes, etc.). Identify, too, anything that might add to the attraction of the area, such as start-ups, research centres, new transport infrastructures or even works carried out by the local council to smarten up the town. And also identify the factors which could diminish the attractiveness of the area, such as the closure of certain key businesses, an increase in petty crime, old or run-down public amenities, or a significant rise in the council's debt.

Once you have assessed the area and found the right locality, the property itself should be in good condition inside and out. In other words, it should be desirable. Identify the ongoing or potential problems by going through the minutes of co-owner meetings. Call on the services of an architect or a building specialist to check the condition of the property. And don't fall into the trap of the latest trick used by estate agents to hide a property's faults: home staging.

Its price must be comparable to the going rate of similar properties on the market, and ideally as much under this price as possible. If it is in poor condition but has potential, integrate the cost of works into your calculations, and don't forget to add a safety margin just in case repairs are more significant or take longer than anticipated. Also take into account uncertainties such as a lowering of the rent index, non-occupation, unpaid rent, collective works (boiler, rendering, etc.) or individual repairs (broken appliances, leaks in the plumbing, etc.), expected or not, tax increases, changes in interest if your mortgage is at a variable rate...

Next, invest a bit of money in expert advice on determining, for example, the most appropriate legal structure, fiscal framework, tax planning strategies, and inheritance regime. An accountant specializing in real estate and an expert tax lawyer are just two of the professionals you should consult before setting yourself up in the real-estate business. They could save you a lot of money in the long run, and help you avoid numerous pitfalls.

Find good tenants by using the services of professionals in the field, and select them on the basis of objective factors, that is to say, don't be swayed by your emotions or personal sentiment. You are in business and must deal in facts. Get a professional to draft the contract and don't hesitate having the final document reviewed by a specialist lawyer before signing. A lawyer is more likely to spot risks that an estate agent could overlook.

If you are not available for managing the day-to-day running of the property (collecting rent, undertaking repairs, keeping accounts, and so on), employ a professional to do it for you. Watch how he or she goes about their business in order to identify tasks that you can undertake yourself to save money. You will also learn the tricks of the trade and become more resilient to being taken for a ride. In the case of a dispute, stay in contact with the legal practitioners who you previously contacted. If you use the services of an estate agent, make sure that the agency has a suitable structure for managing disputes efficiently. And don't forget to take out insurance cover for unpaid rent and other risks that you won't necessarily have anticipated.

Ignore no risk and be prepared for every eventuality, especially since you have decided to play the card of leveraged investing. Always have a financial safety net to help you deal with the uncertainties. You should be able to weather periods of non-occupation, unexpected works, one-off charges, various disputes and other risks which have the potential to turn your investment into a disaster – and even cause your financial ruin.

If you aren't familiar with the workings of property investment, you will need to learn. And there is a lot to learn. It will cost you time and money, not for spending but for investing in your project and in your capacity for bringing it to fruition.

Conclusion

Do you remember what I wrote about at the start of this book? I talked about unemployment, stress and physically demanding work. And the book ends with a description of a possible future where you can enjoy yourself, undertake personal projects, live more peacefully, work for yourself and for those you love.

It is exactly what my career allowed me to achieve and I wanted to share that experience with you. I cannot guarantee that my experiences and the lessons I drew from them, in particular those that I have shared with you, are the ingredients of a universal recipe for success. That would be impossible. I hope nevertheless that they help you keep your job, develop your career and above all get the best out of your life by being proactive and not passively accepting your fate.

This book has dealt with many and various points. Some might say it is a hotchpotch of ideas. And they would be right, in a way. I have realized that all these factors are part of a greater whole. If one of them is missing, just like an ingredient omitted from a cake recipe, the result will probably be disappointing. And all these factors interact in a similar way to the ingredients in a recipe. There is a cumulative effect which comes into play and which, at a certain stage that you can't really predict, sets you on the road to success. How does it work? I don't know.

Don't project unrealistic attributes on the workplace and the world around us. Living in your imagination will lull you into a false sense of security, but it won't protect you from pain and suffering, and if you choose this road, you will probably waste your chances in life. Don't live in your dreams. And don't give up on your dreams, either. Turn them into goals that you can achieve. By doing this, you will benefit from greater motivation and greater happiness. By being conscious of the reality of things, by setting yourself clear objectives, by developing a solid mindset, by increasing expertise continuously, and by creating time for yourself, you will be giving yourself every chance of achieving success. You will no longer be just hoping, but instead capable of taking effective action and that will make all the difference.

You will have seized every opportunity to protect your job, and to obtain more fulfilling and better paid positions. You will also have seized every opportunity for making your financial independence no longer a talking point, no longer a dream, but a reality. It will finally be within your grasp.

You will take control of your time. You will no longer waste it and, as a result, you will no longer be wasting your life away. You will become the master of your life. It is an absolutely unique feeling which tips the balance of your life from floundering insecurity into a state of calm, personal well-being and pride in being yourself.

If I have been able to do it and if others have done it, then you can do it too. Your career will become a veritable adventure. You will experience joy and enthusiasm, as well as demotivation and difficulty, that is unavoidable. You will certainly feel like jacking it all in, but you will hang in there. Calm, personal well-being and pride in being yourself need to be earned. They aren't obtained through luck or hope, but only through taking action.

By reading this book you have taken one such action.

It is now time to move on to the next ones.

Be happy. That is the best outcome you could wish for.

Great Midlands
PUBLISHING

Bibliography

Dalio, Ray, *Principles: Life & Work*, Simon & Schuster, 2017

Schroeder, Alice, *The Snowball: Warren Buffett and the Business of Life*, Valor, 2009

Kiyosaki, Robert T., *Rich Dad Poor Dad*, Plata Publishing, 2017

Kiyosaki, Robert T., *Cashflow Quadrant*, Plata Publishing, 2015

Buffett, Warren, *The Essays of Warren Buffett*, The Cunningham Group & Carolina Academic Press, 2015

Branson, Richard, *Screw It, Let's Do It: Lessons In Life*, Virgin Books, 2006

Branson, Richard, *Like a Virgin: Secrets They Won't Teach You at Business School*, Portfolio, 2012

Churchill, Winston, *The Gathering Storm*, Penguin Classics, 2005

Aurelius, Marcus, *Meditations*, Penguin Classics, 2006

Sun Tzu, *The Art of War*, Penguin Classics, 2014

Schopenhauer, Arthur, *The Art of Always Being Right*, Gibson Square Books, 2006

Van Vogt, Alfred E., *The Voyage of the Space Beagle*, Orb Books, 2008

Isaacson, Walter, *Steve Jobs*, Simon & Schuster, 2011

Belfort, Jordan, *Way of the Wolf: Straight Line Selling*, Gallery Books, 2017

Orwell, George, *Animal Farm*, Penguin, 2003

Published by Great Midlands Publishing Ltd, London

Great Midlands
PUBLISHING

www.ingramcontent.com/pod-product-compliance
Lightning Source LLC
LaVergne TN
LVHW052109210926
848482LV00024B/388
* 9 7 8 1 9 1 6 7 0 2 1 7 2 *